TWO ESSAYS
ON
THE MIND

Painting of Benjamin Rush by Adele von Helmhold
(after T. Sully) reproduced by courtesy of the
College of Physicians of Philadelphia

BENJAMIN RUSH, M.D.

TWO ESSAYS
ON
THE MIND

An Enquiry into THE INFLUENCE of PHYSICAL CAUSES UPON THE MORAL FACULTY

AND

On the INFLUENCE OF PHYSICAL CAUSES IN PROMOTING AN INCREASE OF THE STRENGTH AND ACTIVITY OF THE INTELLECTUAL FACULTIES OF MAN

Introduction by
ERIC T. CARLSON, M.D.

BRUNNER/MAZEL, *Publishers* • New York • 1972

The publishers wish to express their grateful appreciation
to the Oskar Diethelm Historical Library of the
New York Hospital-Cornell Medical Center for
their cooperation in permitting reproduction
of these two essays from the first edition
copies in their collection.

Copyright © 1972 by Brunner/Mazel, Inc.
64 University Place, New York, N. Y. 10003
Library of Congress Catalog Card Number 72-86299
Manufactured in the United States of America
SBN 87630-061-1

INTRODUCTION

The two essays presented in this volume, reproduced from their original texts, illustrate some of Dr. Rush's mature thought on faculty psychology. As they were written in 1786 and 1799 respectively, the essays cannot be judged fairly in modern terms but must be seen in their historical context. If examined in this light these essays highlight the structure of Rush's thinking on the influence of physiological causes on the moral and intellectual faculties of man, in both normal and disordered functioning. (1)

1786, the year in which Dr. Benjamin Rush delivered the first of the two essays in this volume, marks the midpoint of the "critical period" (1781-1789) in American government. Following Lord Cornwallis' surrender to General Washington at Yorktown, October 1781, the emerging American nation operated under the Articles of Confederation as interpreted through the Continental Congress. Territorial disputes, widespread land inflation and monetary uncertainty nagged the federation, eroding national confidence and threatening national pride. Impelled by this new American crisis, Benjamin Franklin petitioned for release from his role as United States Ambassador Plenipotentiary in France and returned to Philadelphia in September, 1785, to continue his efforts as political reformer and cultural guardian of the American states.

In 1743, Franklin had offered "A Proposal for promoting useful knowledge among the British Plantations in America" which led to the founding of the American Philosophical Society that same year. A competing group, The American Society held at Philadelphia for Promoting Useful Knowledge (of which Dr. Rush was a member), merged into the senior organization in 1769, under the single title of the American Philosophical Society. Soon after his return to Philadelphia in 1785, Franklin renewed his efforts to revitalize their programs; like most organizations, its activities had suffered during the war. Accordingly, at the December 2, 1785, meeting of the Society, Dr. Benjamin Rush was invited to deliver the 1786 Annual Oration; he readily agreed and Monday, February 27, 1786 was fixed as the date (2). Newspaper announcements advertised the occasion for which one thousand tickets were printed; direct invitations were delivered to both the Executive Council and Assembly of the State of Pennsylvania.

On the appointed date, fourteen members of the Society, led by President Benjamin Franklin and Treasurer Francis Hopkinson, met with Dr. Rush to begin the formal procession across cobblestoned Independence Square to the Hall of the College of Philadelphia. Here, at 7:00 P.M., Benjamin Rush delivered his Oration: *"An Enquiry into the Influence of Physical Causes upon the Moral Faculty"* before "a very respectable assembly of Gentlemen and ladies convened for the purpose." At the request of the Society, Dr. Rush published his Oration in 1786 (3); it remains a milestone in American psychiatric development (4).

Dr. Rush was born to John and Susanna (Hall Harvey) Rush in 1746, fourth of their seven children (5). Five years later John Rush died, leaving his family but slight financial means and a deep sense of loss. With characteristic energy and singleness of purpose, Susanna Rush was able to provide for her family from the proceeds of a grocery store she opened in Philadelphia, determined to provide each child, male and female, with a strong education. In 1753, she sent Benjamin to the Nottingham (Pennsylvania) school opened by her brother-in-law, the Reverend Samuel Finley, and from there to the College of New Jersey (now Princeton University), where Reverend Finley held the Office of President, 1761-1766.

Rejecting his initial attraction to the legal profession, Rush decided instead on a medical career and in the autumn of 1760 was apprenticed to the renowned Philadelphia physician, John Redman. Toward the close of this five-year period, Rush attended several medical courses at the newly-founded College of Philadelphia. (This institution, the first American medical school, continues today as the University of Pennsylvania.) Energetic and ambitious, Rush left Philadelphia for Scotland in August 1766 to enroll at the medical school of the University of Edinburgh, where he studied for two terms under Dr. William Cullen, a dominant figure in 18th-century European medicine. In 1768 and 1769, Rush visited London and Paris, completing his medical studies there before returning to Philadelphia in July 1769.

In August of that year, Dr. Rush was elected Professor of Chemistry in the College of Philadelphia. The popularity and scope of his teachings, his years of effort to further the study of this field, and his publication of the first native chemistry syllabus have earned for him the title of "Father of American Chemistry." He continued to deliver lectures on this scientific discipline until 1789, when he accepted the professorship of Theory and Practice of Medicine. Two years later, during a period of reorganization at the newly-named University of Pennsylvania, Rush was offered the additional professorship of the Institutes of Medicine. (This is a 17th-century term for the study of physiology, popularized by the eminent Dutch physician, Herman Boerhaave; William Cullen held this professorship at the University of Edinburgh during Rush's student days there.)

Rush entered his new appointment enthusiastically: "I began to prepare for the duties of my new Professorship by reading Boerhaave, Dr. Haller, Hunter, Gregory, Cullen's manuscript lectures, and many small tracts upon physiological subjects. From none of them did I derive so many useful hints as from Dr. Hartley's treatise upon the frame of man. About a week before the meeting of the classes, I sat down to compose my lectures, and during the winter in the midst of constant business, I finished and delivered a course of lectures upon the Institutes of Medicine. Never before had I stretched my faculties to such an extent. I slept but little, and lived sparingly during this severe paroxysm of bodily and mental exertion" (6). During succeeding years, it was Dr. Rush's custom to deliver an Introductory Lecture before the assembled medical students in Surgeons' Hall. The second essay in this volume, *"On the Influence of Physical Causes, in Promoting an Increase of the Strength and Activity of the Intellectual Faculties of Man,"* originally composed Rush's ninth Introduction (November 18, 1799) (7) to his course of lectures on physiology given at the College of Philadelphia.

These lectures on physiology contain Dr. Rush's theories of what we now call physiological psychology and faculty psychology (8). The inclusion of these studies is not original with Rush; a similar trend was developing in the lectures of both Boerhaave and Cullen. But the importance Rush places on this subject was new for his time. He states, "[Knowledge of the mind] should be the vade mecum of every physician. It opens to him many new duties. It is calculated to teach him, that in feeling the pulse, inspecting the eyes and tongue, examining the state of the excretions, he performs but half his duty in a sick room. To render his prescriptions successful, he should pry into the state of his patient's mind, and so regulate his conduct and conversation as to aid the operation of his physical remedies." He continues, "Besides the advantages which a physician may derive from a knowledge of the faculties and operations of the mind in furnishing him with numerous and powerful articles of the materia medica, he will find it useful in predicting the issue of diseases in life or death" (9).

Rush's psychology was most strongly influenced by the eminent British philosopher, David Hartley (10). Hartley meshed the 18th-century concepts of motion and Newtonian physics into his theory of the nervous system wherein he postulated that vibrations of minute particles of nervous ether caused nervous impulses which resulted in communication. According to Hartley, the mind is a "tabula rasa" on which these vibrations project perceptions; through the process of association, these perceptions fill the mind with ideas (11). Rush abstracted this vibrations concept into simple motion, and made association but one of his six operations of the mind.

Patterning his theory after the Scottish school of mental philosophy, Rush postulated that there existed in the mind certain basic capacities or faculties. These faculties were innate but could be stimulated into action and growth. Following Aristotelian terminology, he called these mental faculties "internal senses." His choice of nine faculties is a considerable extension of the traditional three: reason, emotion and will, but falls far below the numbers given by the Scottish School. Rush grouped these nine faculties into three categories: the moral faculties included the moral faculty proper, conscience, and sense of deity; the intellectual faculties incorporated understanding, memory, and imagination. The remaining three were the passions, will, and the principle of faith (the "believing faculty"). Each faculty had separate powers but coordinated with the other eight. This type of theory, when combined with the idea that each faculty was represented by a separate area in the brain, secured popular acceptance in the 19th century as Phrenology—a term Rush may have introduced, not for the movement but to designate his own medical psychology (12).

A word should be said about Rush's medical theory which appears in more detailed form in the second essay. As stated previously, William Cullen exerted a strong influence on Rush during his Edinburgh years. Utilizing the nervous system as the center of bodily force, and the capacity of the body to respond to this force with varying degrees of irritability or sensibility (i.e., motion and sensation), Cullen's system employed the modern-day concept of stimulus-response. Gradually, Rush evolved his own concept of bodily force, and brought it to completion during the years immediately preceding 1795. He perceived life as a forced state caused by stimuli; these stimuli acted upon the body's capacity to respond (excitability) and created the motion (excitement) that functioned as the life force. When a stimulus produced an irregular or convulsive excitement, disease resulted. Thus, for Rush, all disease had a unitary cause (disordered excitement); the blood vessels, specifically the arteries, served as the main organ system in the control and distribution of this excitement.

Accordingly, madness was caused by an irregular action of the arteries of the brain.

Though parallel in outline and development, there is a difference in focus between the two essays. In the moral Inquiry Rush demonstrates that moral faculties are subject to derangement, while in his Introduction on the intellectual faculties he shows how those faculties can be strengthened and improved in their functioning. Not until 1812, a year before his death, did Rush publish the text of his mature theory of mental illness, *Medical Inquiries and Observations upon the Diseases of the Mind*. He divided intellectual derangement into two main types: partial insanity and general intellectual disorder. Partial insanity with disturbed thinking or delusion took one of two forms: tristimania (hypochondriasis or amenomania (melancholia). General intellectual derangement was to be found in cases of delirium and phrenitis and, most typically, in the acute forms of mania. Diseases of the memory included conditions we now would term aphasia and the more general defects of diffuse cerebral disturbance seen in aging. Younger persons afflicted with memory impairment were diagnosed as suffering from fatuity or idiotism. Rush dealt only sparingly with disturbances of the imagination.

Disturbances of the intellectual faculties had long been accepted as proper subject for medical speculation and classification but the same had not been the case for the moral faculties. Rush tried to make his presentation more generally acceptable to those who took issue with his theories on philosophic and religious grounds by producing parallel examples of similar derangements of the two faculty groups. He termed this process "analogy," a method of verification popular with Rush, who never really accepted the more exacting scientific method which was gaining ascendancy. The cases discussed are largely those included in modern rubric under "personality disorders," including such problems as stealing, lying, opium addiction, alcoholism, suicide and murder. Perhaps his best illustration of "anomia" (i.e., a total absence of the moral faculty, to be distinguished from "micronomia," or a weakening of this faculty) is taken not from his clinical experiences but from literature—the character of Servin. Servin was charming, talented, brilliant and creative, and, an unscrupulous rogue. "He was treacherous, cruel, cowardly, deceitful, a liar, a cheat, a drunkard, and a glutton, a sharper in play, immersed in every species of vice, a blasphemer, an atheist." To say such a person was ill and not immoral challenged both the mores and medical concepts of the day.

Not surprisingly, Rush had to plead for attention and tolerance: "We bestow much study and great labor in restoring the wandering reason of our fellow creatures; but we neglect their erring hearts. We erect splendid and commodious buildings to confine persons, when intellectual derangement has rendered them dangerous to society, and we employ our skill and humanity to relieve them; but with an unmerciful impatience, we consign persons, whom moral derangement has rendered mischievous, to the exterminating ax and halter" (13).

In his writings, Rush made early and largely-unrecognized contributions to the understanding of behavioral disorders. James Cowles Prichard is generally credited with popularizing the study of moral insanity, based on his work of 1835 in which he introduced the term. This subject served as the focus of psychological studies and polemical arguments until replaced by the category of psychopathic personality at the end of the century (14).

As a product of the 18th century, Rush shared a common belief in our capacity for human progress; his efforts on behalf of educational reform as the means for achieving this advancement involved most of the culturally-unexposed groups of his time: Indians, the poor, slaves, and women. His concern with the mental faculties, intellectual and moral, of these essays was not limited to his role as physician; as a reformer, he sought to spread an understanding of their roles in the functioning of the total person, and to give all persons the opportunity to develop them to maximum capacity. These reform efforts covered many areas. In government, Dr. Rush was a Signer of the Declaration of Independence, actively campaigned for ratification of the Constitution, and proposed establishing a cabinet post for a Secretary of Peace; he agitated for penal reform and the abolition of capital punishment. Dr. Rush was against tyranny in any form—repressive government, enslavement of blacks (15), or the slavery induced by alcoholism. He believed that poverty bred its own form of slavery, through ill-health and ignorance. He started his medical practice among the poor and maintained a life-long interest in their welfare; he was instrumental in opening the first free medical dispensary in the United States in 1786, the Philadelphia Dispensary. Appointed in 1783 to the Pennsylvania Hospital (the first hospital in the American colonies, founded 1752), he worked during the next thirty years for improvements in the care and treatment of the insane. The impact of these efforts, his psychiatric teachings, and his previously-mentioned publication of the first native textbook on this subject have earned for Benjamin Rush a secure position in the history of psychiatry in America, symbolized by his portrait on the seal of the American Psychiatric Association.

Stylistically, Rush's essays are lively and entertaining; his illustrations charm the reader and suggest applications that are meaningful today. Textually, they are not open to penetrating scrutiny for philosophical depth; critical reading often reveals an inner contradiction. But Rush's goal was that of practical and popular dissemination of his thought and not one of intricate reasonings. When studied in the light of Dr. Rush's own goals when writing them, these essays reflect one man's honest attempts to understand the basic nature and problems of man, goals that are equally noble today.

ERIC T. CARLSON, M.D.
Clinical Professor of Psychiatry
Section on the History of Psychiatry
and the Behavioral Sciences
The New York Hospital—Cornell Medical Center

REFERENCES

1. The author wishes to thank Beatrice T. Heveran for her editorial assistance and to acknowledge the support in part of a Research Grant from the National Science Foundation. (GS198)

2. *Early Proceedings of the American Philosophical Society ... from the Manuscript Minutes of Its Meetings from 1744 to 1838*, Philadelphia: McCalla and Stavely, 1884, pp. 135 and 141.

3. RUSH, BENJAMIN, *An Oration, delivered before the American Philosophical Society, held in Philadelphia on the 27th of February, 1786; containing an Enquiry into the Influence of Physical Causes upon the Moral Faculty ...*, Philadelphia: Charles Cist, 1786. In the same year a second edition was published in London by a friend of Rush (Philadelphia, Printed: London, Reprinted; for C. Dilly, 1786).

4. CARLSON, ERIC T. & MERIBETH M. SIMPSON, "Benjamin Rush's Medical Use of the Moral Faculty," *Bulletin of the History of Medicine*, 1965, 39:22-33.

5. Two good accounts of Rush's life exist: Nathan G. Goodman's *Benjamin Rush: Physician and Citizen, 1746-1813*, Philadelphia: University of Pennsylvania Press, 1934, gives an excellent picture of Rush's intellectual life, while a more readable humanistic biography is Carl Binger's *Revolutionary Doctor: Benjamin Rush, 1746-1813*, New York: W. W. Norton and Co., 1966.

   Further information may be found in Lyman H. Butterfield (Ed.) *Letters of Benjamin Rush*, 2 vols., Princeton: Princeton University Press for the American Philosophical Society, 1951 and in Rush's Autobiography. (See Reference 6.)

6. CORNER, GEORGE (Ed.) *The Autobiography of Benjamin Rush*, Princeton: Princeton University Press for the American Philosophical Society, 1948, p. 94.

7. This essay was printed first in *Six Introductory Lectures, to Courses of Lectures, upon the Institutes and Practice of Medicine, delivered in the University of Pennsylvania*, Philadelphia: John Conrad, 1801 and reprinted in *Sixteen Introductory Lectures to Courses of Lectures upon the Institutes and Practice of Medicine, with a Syllabus of the Latter*, Philadelphia: Bradford and Innskeep, 1811.

8. RUSH, BENJAMIN, *A Syllabus of a Course of Lectures on the Institutes of Medicine*, Philadelphia: Parry Hall, 1792.

9. *Sixteen Introductory Lectures, op. cit.*, pp. 266 and 268.

10. D'ELIA, DONALD J., "Benjamin Rush, David Hartley, and the Revolutionary Uses of Psychology," *Proc. Am. Phil. Soc.*, 1970, 114:109-118.

11. HARTLEY, DAVID, *Observations on Man, His Frame, His Duty, and His Expectations*, (1749) 3 vols., London: J. Johnson, 1801. Fourth edition.

12. NOEL, PATRICIA S. & ERIC T. CARLSON, "Origins of the Word 'Phrenology'," *Am. J. Psychiat.*, 1970, 127:649-697.

13. *Sixteen Introductory Lectures, op. cit.*, p. 393.

14. CARLSON, ERIC T. & NORMAN DAIN, "The Meaning of Moral Insanity," *Bull. Hist. Med.*, 1962, 36:130-140.

15. D'ELIA, DONALD, "Dr. Benjamin Rush and the Negro," *J. Hist. Ideas*, 1969, 30:413-422, and Plummer, Betty L., "Benjamin Rush and the Negro," *Am. J. Psychiat.*, 1970, 127:793-798.

CONTENTS

	Page
INTRODUCTION	v

An Enquiry into the Influence of Physical
    Causes upon the Moral Faculty (1786) 1

On the Influence of Physical Causes in Promoting
    an Increase of the Strength and Activity
    of the Intellectual Faculties of Man (1799) 41

AN ORATION,

DELIVERED BEFORE THE

AMERICAN PHILOSOPHICAL SOCIETY,

HELD IN PHILADELPHIA ON THE 27th OF FEBRUARY, 1786;

CONTAINING

An Enquiry into the INFLUENCE of PHYSICAL CAUSES upon the MORAL FACULTY.

By BENJAMIN RUSH, M. D.

AND PROFESSOR OF CHEMISTRY IN THE UNIVERSITY OF PENNSYLVANIA.

HUMAN KNOWLEDGE, under the present circumstances of our beings and Constitutions, may be carried much further than it has hitherto been, if men would employ all their industry, and labor of thought, in improving the means of discovering truth.

MORALITY is the science, and business of mankind.   LOCKE.

PHILADELPHIA:
PRINTED BY CHARLES CIST. M,DCC,LXXXVI

TO

HIS EXCELLENCY

BENJAMIN FRANKLIN, Esq.

PRESIDENT

OF THE

SUPREME EXECUTIVE COUNCIL

OF

PENNSYLVANIA,

THE FRIEND AND BENEFACTOR

OF

MANKIND,

THE FOLLOWING ORATION IS RESPECTFULLY INSCRIBED,

BY HIS GRATEFUL FRIEND,
AND HUMBLE SERVANT,
THE AUTHOR.

PREFACE.

MOST of the facts, together with the principles contained in the following Oration, were committed to paper above seven years ago.——If, they have the same operation upon the mind of the reader, that they had upon the mind of the author, they will at first be doubted——afterwards believed, and finally they will be propagated. He is so far from proposing physical influence, as a substitute for religious, moral, or rational instruction, that he offers it only as a reinforcement to the obligations of reason and religion; or rather, as a neglected part of christianity. He is sensible that in this new, and difficult enquiry, he has only performed the drudgery of a pioneer: Those who come after him upon this subject, will find a way opened, for extensive and important observations, and will probably enjoy with more certainty, than the author, the fruits of their labors.

At a Meeting of the American Philosophical Society, February 27th, 1786.

On motion, *Resolved unanimously*, That the Thanks of the Society be given to Dr. Benjamin Rush, for his Oration, " On the Influence of Physical Causes on the Moral Faculty," delivered before the Society this Evening, and that the Secretaries be directed to request the Doctor to furnish them with a Copy of the said Oration for Publication.

Extract from the Minutes,
JAMES HUTCHINSON, *Secretary.*

GENTLEMEN,

IT was for the laudable purpose of exciting a spirit of emulation and enquiry, among the members of our body, that the founders of our Society, instituted an annual oration. The task of preparing, and delivering this exercise, hath devolved, once more, upon me. I have submitted to it,—not because I thought myself capable of fulfilling your intentions, but because I wished, by a testimony of my obedience to your requests, to atone for my long absence from the temple of science.

The subject upon which I am to have the honor of addressing you this evening, is "An enquiry into the influence of physical " causes upon the moral faculty."

By the moral faculty I mean a power in the human mind of distinguishing and chusing good and evil; or, in other words, virtue and vice. It is a native principle, and though it is capable of improvement by experience and reflection, it is not derived from either of them.———St. Paul, and Cicero, give us the most perfect account of it that is to be found in modern or ancient authors. " For when the Gentiles, (says St. Paul) which have not the law, " do by nature the things contained in the law, *these*, having not " the law, are a *law* unto themselves; which shew the works of
" the

" the law written in their hearts, their consciences also bearing
" witness, and their thoughts the mean while accusing, or else
" excusing one another*."

The words of Cicero are as follow——" Est igitur hæc, judices,
" non scripta, sed nata lex, quam non didicimus, accepimus, legi-
" mus, verum ex natura ipsa arripuimus, hausimus, expressimus,
" ad quam non docti, sed facti, non instituti, sed imbuti sumus."†
This faculty is often confounded with conscience, which is a
distinct and independent power of the mind. This is evident from
the passage quoted from the writings of St. Paul, in which conscience is said to be the witness that accuses, or excuses us, of a
breach of the law written in our hearts. The moral faculty is what
the schoolmen call the " regula regulans,"—the conscience is their
" regula regulata." Or, to speak in more modern terms, the
moral faculty performs the office of a law-giver, while the business
of conscience is to perform the duty of a judge. The moral
faculty is to the conscience, what taste is to the judgment, and sensation to perception. It is quick in its operations, and like the
sensitive plant, acts without reflection, while conscience follows with
deliberate steps, and measures all her actions, by the unerring square
of right and wrong. The moral faculty exercises itself upon the
actions of others. It approves even in books, of the virtues of a
Trajan, and disapproves of the vices of a Marius, while conscience
confines its operations, only to its own actions. These two powers
of the mind are generally in an exact ratio to each other, but they
sometimes exist in different degrees in the same person. Hence we
often

* Rom. II. 14. 15.
† Oratio pro Milone.

often find confcience in its full vigor, with a diminifhed tone, or total abfence of the moral faculty.

It has long been a queftion among metaphyficians, whether the confcience be feated in the will or in the underftanding. The controverfy can only be fettled by admitting the will to be the feat of the moral faculty, and the underftanding to be the feat of the confcience. The myfterious nature of the union of thofe two moral principles with the will and underftanding, is a fubject foreign to the bufinefs of the prefent enquiry.———

As I confider virtue and vice to confift in *action*, and not in opinion, and as this action has its feat in the *will*, and not in the confcience, I fhall confine my enquiries chiefly to the influence of phyfical caufes upon that moral power of the mind, which is connected with volition, although many of thefe caufes act likewife upon the confcience, as I fhall fhew hereafter.———The ftate of the moral faculty is vifible in actions, which affect the well-being of fociety. The ftate of the confcience is invifible, and therefore removed beyond our inveftigation.

The moral faculty has received different names from different authors. It is the "moral fenfe" of Dr. Hutchifon——the "fympathy" of Dr. Adam Smith——the "moral inftinct" of Roufieau——and "the light that lighteth every man that cometh into the world" of St. John. I have adopted the term of moral faculty from Dr. Beattie, becaufe I conceive ~~they~~ convey with the moft perfpicuity, the idea of a power in the mind, of chufing good and evil.

Our books of medicine contain many records of the effects of physical causes upon the memory—the imagination—and the judgement. In some instances we behold their operation only on one,—in others on two,—and in many cases upon the whole of these faculties. Their derangement has received different names, according to the number or nature of the faculties that are affected. The loss of memory has been called "amnesia"—false judgment upon one subject has been called "melancholia"—false judgment upon all subjects has been called "mania"—and a defect of all the three intellectual faculties that have been mentioned, has received the name of "amentia." Persons who labour under the derangement, or want of these powers of the mind, are considered, very properly, as subjects of medicine; and there are many cases upon record that prove, that their diseases have yielded to the healing art.

In order to illustrate the effects of physical causes upon the moral faculty, it will be necessary *first* to shew their effects upon the memory—the imagination—and the judgment; and at the same time to point out the analogy between their operation upon the intellectual powers of the mind, and the moral faculty.

1. Do we observe a connection between the intellectual powers, and the degrees of consistency and firmness of the brain in infancy and childhood?———The same connection has been observed between the strength as well as the progress of the moral faculty in children.

2. Do we observe a certain size of the brain, and a peculiar cast of features, such as the prominent eye, and the aquiline nose, to be connected with extraordinary portions of genius?———We observe a
similar

similar connection between the figure and temperament of the body, and certain moral faculties.——Hence we often ascribe good temper and benevolence to corpulency, and irascibility to sanguineous habits. Cæsar thought himself safe in the friendship of the "sleek-headed" Anthony and Dolabella, but was afraid to trust to the professions of the slender Cassius.

3. Do we observe certain degrees of the intellectual faculties to be hereditary in certain families? The same observation has been frequently extended to moral qualities——Hence we often find certain virtues and vices as peculiar to families, through all their degrees of consanguinity, and duration, as a peculiarity of voice—complexion—or shape.

4. Do we observe instances of a total want of memory——imagination—and judgment, either from an original defect in the stamina of the brain, or from the influence of physical causes?—— The same unnatural defect is sometimes observed, and probably from the same causes, of a moral faculty. The celebrated Servin, whose character is drawn by the Duke of Sully in his memoirs, appears to be an instance of the total absence of the moral faculty, while the chasm, produced thereby in his mind, seems to have been filled up by a more than common extension of every other power of his mind. I shall beg leave to repeat the history of this prodigy of vice and knowledge.——" Let the reader represent to
" himself a man of a genius so lively, and of an understanding so
" extensive, as rendered him scarce ignorant of any thing that
" could be known——of so vast and ready a comprehension, that
" he immediately made himself master of whatever he attempted,—
" and

" and of so prodigious a memory, that he never forgot what he
" once learned. He possessed all parts of philosophy, and the
" mathematics, particularly fortification and drawing. Even in
" theology he was so well skilled, that he was an excellent
" preacher, whenever he had a mind to exert that talent, and an
" able disputant, for and against the reformed religion indifferently.
" He not only understood Greek—Hebrew—and all the languages
" which we call learned, but also all the different jargons, or
" modern dialects. He accented and pronounced them so naturally,
" and so perfectly imitated the gestures and manners both of the
" several nations of Europe, and the particular provinces of France,
" that he might have been taken for a native of all, or of any of
" these countries: and this quality he applied to counterfeit all
" sorts of persons, wherein he succeeded wonderfully. He was
" moreover the best comedian, and the greatest droll that perhaps
" ever appeared. He had a genius for poetry, and had wrote
" many verses. He played upon almost all instruments—was a
" perfect master of music—and sung most agreeably and justly.
" He likewise could say mass, for he was of a disposition to do,
" as well as to know, all things. His body was perfectly well
" suited to his mind. He was light, nimble, and dexterous, and
" fit for all exercises. He could ride well, and in dancing, wrest-
" ling, and leaping, he was admired. There are not any recreative
" games that he did not know, and he was skilled in almost all
" mechanic arts. But now for the reverse of the medal. Here it
" appeared, that he was treacherous—cruel—cowardly—deceitful—
" a liar—a cheat—a drunkard and a glutton—a sharper in play—
" immersed in every species of vice—a blasphemer—an atheist.——
" In a word—in him might be found all the vices that are contrary

" to

" to nature—honor—religion—and society,——the truth of which
" he himself evinced with his latest breath; for he died in the
" flower of his age, in a common brothel, perfectly corrupted by
" his debaucheries, and expired with the glass in his hand, cursing,
" and denying God."*

It was probably a state of the human mind such as has been described, that our Saviour alluded to in the disciple, who was about to betray him, when he called him "a devil." Perhaps the essence of depravity in infernal spirits, consists in their being wholly devoid of a moral faculty. In them the will has probably lost the power of chusing, † as well as the inclination of enjoying moral good. It is true, we read of their trembling in a belief of the existence of a God, and of their anticipating future punishment by asking, whether they were to be tormented before their time: But this is the effect of conscience, and hence arises another argument in favor of this judicial power of the mind, being distinct from the moral faculty. It would seem as if the Supreme Being had preserved the moral faculty in man from the ruins of his fall, on purpose to guide him back again to Paradise, and at the same time had constituted the conscience, both in men and in fallen spirits, a kind of royalty in his moral empire, on purpose to shew his property in all intelligent creatures, and their original resemblance to himself. Perhaps the essence

of

---

* Vol. III. p. 216. 217.

† Milton seems to have been of this opinion. Hence, after ascribing repentance to Satan, he makes him declare,

" Farewell remorse: all good to me is lost,
" *Evil* be thou, my *good*."———

PARADISE LOST, Book IV.

of moral depravity in man consists in a total, but temporary suspension of the power of conscience. Persons in this situation are emphatically said in the scriptures to be "past feeling"——and to have their consciences seared, with a "hot iron"——they are likewise said to be "twice dead"——that is, the same torpor or moral insensibility, has seized both the moral faculty and the conscience.

5. Do we ever observe instances of the existence of only *one* of the three intellectual powers of the mind that have been named, in the absence of the other two? We observe something of the same kind with respect to the moral faculty. I once knew a man, who discovered no one mark of reason, who possessed the moral sense or faculty in so high a degree, that he spent his whole life in acts of benevolence. He was not only inoffensive, (which is not always the case with idiots) but he was kind, and affectionate to every body. He had no ideas of time, but what were suggested to him by the returns of the stated periods for public worship, in which he appeared to take great delight. He spent several hours of every day in devotion, in which he was so careful to be private, that he was once found in the most improbable place in the world for that purpose, viz. in an oven.

6. Do we observe the memory, the imagination and the judgment, to be affected by diseases, particularly by fevers, and madness? Where is the physician, who has not seen the moral faculty affected from the same causes! How often do we see the temper wholly changed by a fit of sickness! And how often do we hear persons of the most delicate virtue, utter speeches in the delirium of a fever,

that

that are offensive to decency, or good manners! I have heard a well attested history of a clergyman of the most exemplary moral character, who spent the last moments of a fever which deprived him both of his reason and his life, in profane cursing and swearing. I once attended a young woman in a nervous fever, who discovered after her recovery, a loss of her former habits of veracity. Her memory (a defect of which, might be suspected of being the cause of this vice) was in every respect as perfect as it was before the attack of the fever,* The instances of immorality in maniacs, who were formerly distinguished for the opposite character, are so numerous, and well known, that it will not be necessary to select any cases, to establish the truth of the proposition contained under this head.

7. Do we observe any of the three intellectual powers that have been named, enlarged by diseases? Patients in the delirium of a fever, often discover extraordinary flights of imagination, and madmen often astonish us with their wonderful acts of memory. The same enlargement, sometimes, appears in the operations of the moral faculty. I have more than once heard the most sublime discourses on morality in the cell of an hospital, and who has not seen instances of patients in acute diseases, discovering degrees of benevolence and integrity, that were not natural to them in the ordinary course of their lives?

C 8. Do

---

* I have selected this case from many others, which have come under my notice, in which the moral faculty appeared to be impaired by diseases, particularly by the typhus of Dr. Cullen, and by those species of palsy which affect the brain.

8. Do we ever observe a partial insanity, or false perception on one subject, while the judgment is sound and correct, upon all others? We perceive, in some instances, a similar defect in the moral faculty. There are persons who are moral in the highest degree, as to certain duties, who nevertheless live under the influence of some one vice. I knew an instance of a woman, who was examplary in her obedience to every command of the moral law, except one. She could not refrain from stealing. What made this vice the more remarkable was, that she was in easy circumstances, and not addicted to extravagance in any thing. Such was her propensity to this vice, that when she could lay her hands upon nothing more valuable, she would often, at the table of a friend, fill her pockets secretly with bread. As a proof that her judgment was not affected by this defect in her moral faculty, she would both confess and lament her crime, when detected in it.

9. Do we observe the imagination in many instances to be affected with apprehensions of dangers that have no existence? In like manner we observe the moral faculty to discover a sensibility to vice, that is by no means proportioned to its degrees of depravity. How often do we see persons labouring under this morbid sensibility of the moral faculty, refuse to give a direct answer to a plain question, that related perhaps only to the weather, or to the hour of the day, lest they should wound the peace of their minds, by telling a falsehood!

10. Do dreams affect the memory—the imagination—and the judgment? Dreams are nothing but incoherent ideas, occasioned by partial or imperfect sleep. There is a variety in the suspension

of the powers of the mind in this state of the system. In some cases the imagination only is deranged in dreams—in others the memory is affected——and in others the judgment. —— But there are cases, in which the change that is produced in the state of the brain, by means of sleep, affects the moral faculty likewise; hence we sometimes dream of doing and saying things when asleep, which we shudder at, as soon as we awake. This supposed defection from virtue, exists frequently in dreams where the memory and judgment are scarcely impaired. It cannot therefore be ascribed to the desertion of those two powers of the mind.

11. Do we read in the accounts of travellers of men, who in respect of intellectual capacity and enjoyments, are but a few degrees above brutes? We read likewise of a similar degradation of our species, in respect to moral capacity and feeling. Here it will be necessary to remark, that the low degrees of moral perception, that have been discovered in certain African and Russian tribes of men, no more invalidate our proposition of the universal and essential existence of a moral faculty in the human mind, than the low state of their intellects prove, that reason is not natural to man. Their perceptions of good and evil are in an exact proportion to their intellectual powers. But I will go further, and admit with Mr. Locke,* that some savage nations are totally devoid of the moral faculty, yet it will by no means follow, that this was the original constitution of their minds. The appetite for certain aliments is uniform among all mankind. Where is the nation and the individual

* Essay concerning the Human Understanding. Book I. Chap. III.

vidual, in their primitive state of health, to whom bread is not agreeable? But if we should find savages, or individuals, whose stomachs have been so disordered by intemperance, as to refuse this simple and wholesome article of diet, shall we assert that this was the original constitution of their appetites?——By no means. As well might we assert, because savages destroy their beauty by painting, and cutting their faces, that the principles of taste do not exist naturally in the human mind. It is with virtue as with fire. It exists in the mind, as fire does in certain bodies in a latent or quiescent state. As collision renders the one sensible, so education renders the other visible. It would be as absurd to maintain, because olives become agreeable to many people from habit, that we have no natural appetites for any other kind of food, as to assert that any part of the human species exist without a moral principle, because in some of them, it has wanted causes to excite it into action, or has been perverted by example. There are appetites that are wholly artificial. There are tastes so entirely vitiated, as to perceive beauty in deformity. There are torpid and unnatural passions. Why, under certain unfavorable circumstances, may there not exist also a moral faculty in a state of sleep, or subject to mistakes?

The only apology I shall make, for presuming to differ from that justly celebrated oracle, who first unfolded to us a map of the intellectual world, shall be, that the eagle eye of genius often darts its views beyond the notice of facts, which are accommodated to the slender organs of perception of men, who possess no other talent, than that of observation.

It

It is not surprising, that Mr. Locke has confounded this moral principle with *reason*, or that Lord Shaftsbury has confounded it with *taste*, since all three of these faculties agree in the objects of their approbation, notwithstanding they exist in the mind independent of each other. The favorable influence which the progress of science and taste has had upon morals, can be ascribed to nothing else, but to the perfect union that subsists in nature between the dictates of reason—of taste—and of the moral faculty. Why has the spirit of humanity made such rapid progress for some years past in the courts of Europe? It is because kings and their ministers have been taught to *reason* upon philosophical subjects.—Why have indecency and profanity been banished from the stage in London and Paris? It is because immorality is an offense against the highly cultivated *taste* of the French and English nations.

It must afford great pleasure to the lovers of virtue, to behold the depth and extent of this moral principle in the human mind. Happily for the human race, the intimations of duty and the road to happiness are not left to the slow operations or doubtful inductions of reason, nor to the precarious decisions of taste! Hence we often find the moral faculty in a state of vigor, in persons in whom reason and taste exist in a weak, or in an uncultivated state. It is worthy of notice likewise, that while *second* thoughts are best in matters of judgment, *first* thoughts are always to be preferred in matters that relate to morality. *Second* thoughts, in these cases, are generally parlies between duty and corrupted inclinations. Hence Rousseau has justly said that "a well regulated moral instinct is the surest guide "to happiness."

It must afford equal pleasure to the lovers of virtue to behold, that our moral conduct and happiness are not committed to the determination of a single legislative power.——The conscience, like a wise and faithful council of revision, performs the office of a check upon the moral faculty, and thus prevents the fatal consequences of immoral actions.

An objection, I foresee, will arise to the doctrine of the influence of physical causes upon the moral faculty, from its being supposed to favor the opinion of the *materiality* of the soul. But I do not see that this doctrine obliges us to decide upon the question of the nature of the soul, any more than the facts which prove the influence of physical causes upon the memory—the imagination—or the judgment. I shall however remark upon this subject, that the writers in favor of the *immortality* of the soul have done that truth great injury, by connecting it necessarily with its *immateriality*. The immortality of the soul depends upon the *will* of the Deity, and not upon the supposed properties of spirit. Matter is in its own nature as immortal as spirit. It is resolvable by heat and mixture into a variety of forms; but it requires the same Almighty hand to annihilate it, that it did to create it. I know of no arguments to prove the immortality of the soul, but such as are derived from the christian revelation.* It would be as reasonable to assert, that the bason of the ocean is immortal, from the greatness of its capacity to hold water; or that we are to live for ever in this world, because we are afraid of dying, as to maintain the immortality

---

* " Life and immortality *are* brought to light *only* through the Gospel." 2 Tim. I. 10.

immortality of the foul, from the greatnefs of its capacity for knowledge and happinefs, or from its dread of annihilation.

Nor let it be fuppofed, from any thing that has been faid, that I entertain an idea of the *neceffary* influence of phyfical caufes upon the freedom of the will. I believe in the prefcience of the Deity, becaufe I conceive this attribute to be infeparable from his perfections; and I believe in the freedom of moral agency in man, becaufe I conceive it to be effential to his nature as a refponfible being. In thofe cafes where the moral faculty is deprived of its freedom, by involuntary difeafes, I conceive that man ceafes as much to be a fubject of moral government, as he does to be a fubject of civil government, when he is deprived by involuntary difeafes, of the ufe of his reafon.

I remarked in the beginning of this difcourfe, that perfons who were deprived of the juft exercife of memory—imagination—or judgment, were proper fubjects of medicine; and that there are many cafes upon record which prove, that the difeafes from the derangement of thefe faculties, have yielded to the healing art.

It is perhaps only becaufe the diforders of the moral faculty, have not been traced to a connection with phyfical caufes, that medical writers have neglected to give them a place in their fyftems of nofology, and that fo few attempts have been hitherto made, to leffen or remove them by phyfical as well as rational and moral remedies.

I shall

I shall not attempt to derive any support to my opinions, from the analogy of the influence of physical causes upon the temper and conduct of brute animals. The facts which I shall produce in favor of the action of these causes upon morals in the human species, will, I hope, render unnecessary the arguments that might be drawn from that quarter.

I am aware, that in venturing upon this subject, I step upon untrodden ground.——I feel as Æneas did, when he was about to enter the gates of Avernus, but without a Sybil to instruct me in the mysteries that are before me. I foresee, that men who have been educated in the mechanical habits of adopting popular or established opinions, will revolt at the doctrine I am about to deliver—while men of sense and genius will hear my propositions with candor, and if they do not adopt them, will commend that boldness of enquiry, that prompted me to broach them.

I shall begin with an attempt to supply the defects of nosological writers, by naming the partial or weakened action of the moral faculty, MICRONOMIA. The total absence of this faculty, I shall call ANOMIA. By the law, referred to in these new genera of vesaniæ, I mean the law of nature written in the human heart, and which we formerly quoted from the writings of St. Paul.

In treating of the effects of physical causes upon the moral faculty, it might help to extend our ideas upon this subject, to reduce virtues and vices to certain species, and to point out the effects of particular causes, upon each particular species of virtue

and

and vice; but this would lead us into a field too extensive for the limits of the present enquiry. I shall only hint at a few cases, and have no doubt but the ingenuity of my auditors will supply my silence, by applying the rest.

It is immaterial, whether the physical causes that are to be enumerated, act upon the moral faculty through the medium of the senses—the passions—the memory—or the imagination. Their influence is equally certain, whether they act as remote, predisposing, or occasional causes.

1. The effects of CLIMATE upon the moral faculty claim our first attention. Not only individuals, but nations, derive a considerable part of their moral, as well as intellectual character, from the different portions they enjoy of the rays of the sun. Revenge—levity timidity—and indolence, tempered with occasional emotions of benevolence, are the moral qualities of the inhabitants of warm climates, while selfishness tempered with sincerity and integrity, form the moral character of the inhabitants of cold countries. The state of the weather, and the seasons of the year also, have a visible effect upon moral sensibility. The month of November, in Great Britain, rendered gloomy by constant fogs and rains, has been thought to favor the perpetration of the worst species of murder, while the vernal sun, in middle latitudes, has been as generally remarked for producing gentleness and benevolence.

2. The effects of DIET upon the moral faculty are more certain, though less attended to, than the effects of climate. " Fullness "of bread," we are told, was one of the predisposing causes of the

vices of the cities of the plain. The fasts so often inculcated among the Jews, were intended to lessen the incentives to vice; for pride—cruelty—and sensuality, are as much the natural consequences of luxury, as apoplexies and palsies. But the *quality* as well as the quantity of aliment, has an influence upon morals; hence we find the moral diseases that have been mentioned, are most frequently the offspring of animal food. The elegant prophet Isaiah seems to have been sensible of this, when he ascribes such salutary effects to a temperate and vegetable diet. "Butter and honey shall " he eat," says he, "*that* he may know to refuse the evil, and to " chuse the good." —— But we have many facts which prove the efficacy of a vegetable diet upon the passions. Dr. Arbuthnot assures us, that he cured several patients of irascible tempers, by nothing but a prescription of this simple and temperate regimen.

3. The effects of CERTAIN DRINKS upon the moral faculty are not less observable, than upon the intellectual powers of the mind. Fermented liquors of a good quality, and taken in a moderate quantity, are favorable to the virtues of candor, benevolence and generosity; but when they are taken in excess, or when they are of a bad quality, and drank even in a moderate quantity, they seldom fail of rousing every latent spark of vice into action. The last of these facts is so notorious, that when a man is observed to be ill-natured or quarrelsome in Portugal, after drinking, it is common in that country to say, that " he has drank bad wine." While occasional fits of intoxication produce ill temper in many people, habitual drunkenness (which is generally produced by distilled
spirits)

spirits) never fails to eradicate veracity and integrity from the human mind. Perhaps this may be the reason why the Spaniards, in ancient times, never admitted a man's evidence in a court of justice, who had been convicted of drunkenness.—— Water is the universal sedative of turbulent passions—it not only promotes a general equanimity of temper, but it composes anger. I have heard several well attested cases, of a draught of cold water having suddenly composed this violent passion, after the usual remedies of reason had been applied to no purpose.

4. EXTREME HUNGER produces the most unfriendly effects upon moral sensibility. It is immaterial, whether it acts by inducing a relaxation of the solids, or an acrimony of the fluids, or by the combined operation of both those physical causes. The Indians in this country whet their appetites for that savage species of war, which is peculiar to them, by the stimulus of hunger; hence, we are told, they always return meagre and emaciated from their military excursions. In civilized life we often behold this sensation an overbalance for the restraints of moral feeling; and perhaps this may be the reason, why poverty, which is the most frequent parent of hunger, disposes so generally to theft; for the character of hunger is taken from that vice——It belongs to it "to break through stone walls." So much does this sensation predominate over reason and moral feeling, that Cardinal De Retz suggests to politicians, never to risk a motion in a popular assembly, however wise or just it may be, immediately before dinner.—— That temper must be uncommonly guarded, which is not disturbed by long abstinence from food. One of the worthiest men I ever knew, who made his breakfast his principal meal, was peevish and disagreeable

difagreeable to his friends and family, from the time he left his bed, 'till he fat down to his morning repaft, after which, chearfulnefs fparkled in his countenance, and he became the delight of all around him.

5. I HINTED formerly, in proving the analogy between the effects of DISEASES upon the intellects, and upon the moral faculty, that the latter was frequently impaired by fevers and madnefs. I beg leave to add further upon this head, that not only fevers and madnefs, but the hyfteria and hypochondriafis, as well as all thofe ftates of the body, whether idiopathic or fymptomatic, which are accompanied with preternatural irritability—fenfibility—torpor—ftupor—or mobility of the nervous fyftem, difpofe to vice, either of the body or of the mind. It is in vain to attack thefe vices with lectures upon morality. They are only to be cured by medicine,—particularly by exercife,—the cold bath,—and by a cold or a warm atmofphere. The young woman, whofe cafe I mentioned formerly, that loft her habit of veracity by a nervous fever, recovered this virtue, as foon as her fyftem recovered its natural tone, from the cold weather which happily fucceeded her fever.

6. IDLENESS is the parent of every vice. It is mentioned in the old teftament as another of the predifpofing caufes of the vices of the cities of the plain. LABOR of all kinds, favors and facilitates the practice of virtue. The country life is a happy life; chiefly, becaufe its laborious employments are favorable to virtue, and unfriendly to vice. It is a common practice, I have been told, for the planters in the Southern States, to confign an houfe flave, who has become vicious from idlenefs, to the drudgery of the field,

in

in order to reform him. The Bridewells and workhouses of all civilized countries prove, that LABOR is not only a very severe, but the most benevolent of all punishments, in as much as it is one of the most suitable means of reformation. Mr. Howard tells us in his history of prisons, that in Holland it is a common saying, " Make men work, and you will make them honest." And over the rasp and spin-house at Grœningen, this sentiment is expressed (he tells us) by a happy motto—

" Vitiorum femina—otium—labore exhauriendum."

The effects of steady labor in early life, in creating virtuous habits, is still more remarkable. The late Anthony Benezet of this city, whose benevolence was the sentinel of the virtue, as well as of the happiness of his country, made it a constant rule in binding out poor children, to avoid putting them into wealthy families, but always preferred masters for them who worked themselves, and who obliged these children to work in their presence. If the habits of virtue, contracted by means of this apprenticeship to labor, are purely mechanical, their effects are, nevertheless, the same upon the happiness of society, as if they flowed from principle. The mind, moreover, when preserved by these means from weeds, becomes a more mellow soil afterwards, for moral and rational improvement.

7. THE effects of EXCESSIVE SLEEP are intimately connected with the effects of idleness, upon the moral faculty,—hence we find that moderate, and even scanty portions of sleep, in every part of the world, have been found to be friendly, not only to health and long life, but in many instances to morality. The practice of the Monks, who often sleep upon a floor, and who generally rise

with the fun, for the fake of mortifying their fenfual appetites, is certainly founded in wifdom, and has often produced the moft falutary moral effects.

8. THE effects of BODILY PAIN upon the moral, are not lefs remarkable than upon the intellectual powers of the mind. The late Dr. Gregory of the univerfity of Edinburgh, ufed to tell his pupils, that he always found his perceptions quicker in a fit of the gout, than at any other time. The pangs which attend the diffolution of the body, are often accompanied with conceptions and expreffions upon the moft ordinary fubjects, that difcover an uncommon elevation of the intellectual powers. The effects of bodily pain are exactly the fame in roufing and directing the moral faculty. Bodily pain, we find, was one of the remedies employed in the old teftament, for extirpating vice and promoting virtue: and Mr. Howard tells us, that he faw it employed fuccefsfully as a means of reformation, in one of the prifons which he vifited. If pain has a phyfical tendency to cure vice, I fubmit it to the confideration of parents and legiflators, whether moderate degrees of corporal punifhments, inflicted for a great length of time, would not be more medicinal in their effects, than the violent degrees of them, which are of fhort duration.

9. Too much cannot be faid in favor of CLEANLINESS, as a phyfical mean of promoting virtue. The writings of Mofes have been called by military men, the beft " orderly book" in the world. In every part of them we find cleanlinefs inculcated with as much zeal, as if it was part of the moral, inftead of the levitical law. Now, it is well known, that the principal defign of every precept

and

and rite of the ceremonial parts of the Jewish religion, was to prevent vice, and to promote virtue. All writers upon the leprosy, take notice of its connection with a certain vice. To this disease gross animal food, particularly swine's flesh, and a dirty skin, have been thought to be predisposing causes——hence the reason, probably, why pork was forbidden, and why ablutions of the body and limbs were so frequently inculcated by the Jewish law. Sir John Pringle's remarks, in his Oration upon Capt. Cook's Voyage, delivered before the Royal Society in London, are very pertinent to this part of our subject.—" Cleanliness (says he) is conducive to " health, but it is not so obvious, that it also tends to good order " and other virtues. Such (meaning the ship's crew) as were " made more cleanly, became more sober,—more orderly,—and " more attentive to duty," Mr. Addison, whose observations are seldom false, and never trifling, tells us, that " several vices, de-" structive both to body and mind, are inconsistent with the habit " of cleanliness."* The benefit to be derived by parents and schoolmasters from attending to these facts, is too obvious to be mentioned.

10. I HOPE I shall be excused in placing SOLITUDE among the physical causes which influence the moral faculty, when I add, that I confine its effects to persons who are irreclaimable by rational or moral remedies. Mr. Howard informs us, that the chaplain of the prison at Liege in Germany assured him, " that " the most refractory and turbulent spirits, became tractable and " submissive, by being closely confined for four or five days."— In bodies that are predisposed to vice, the stimulus of cheerful, but much more of profane society and conversation, upon the animal

spirits,

---

* Spectator, No. 631.

spirits, becomes an exciting cause, and like the stroke of the flint upon the steel, renders the sparks of vice both active and visible. By removing men out of the reach of this exciting cause, they are often reformed, especially if they are confined long enough to produce a sufficient chasm in their habits of vice. Where the benefit of reflection, and instruction from books, can be added to solitude and confinement, their good effects are still more certain. To this philosophers and poets in every age have assented, by describing the life of a hermit as a life of passive virtue.

11. CONNECTED with solitude, as a mechanical means of promoting virtue, SILENCE deserves to be mentioned in this place. The late Dr. Fothergill, in his plan of education for that benevolent institution at Ackworth, which was the last care of his useful life, says every thing that can be said in favor of this necessary discipline, in the following words. " To habituate children from
" their early infancy, to silence and attention, is of the greatest ad-
" vantage to them, not only as a preparative to their advancement
" in a religious life, but as the groundwork of a well cultivated
" understanding. To have the active minds of children put under
" a kind of restraint—to be accustomed to turn their attention
" from external objects, and habituated to a degree of abstracted
" quiet, is a matter of great consequence, and lasting benefit to
" them. Although it cannot be supposed, that young and active
" minds are always engaged in silence as they ought to be, yet to
" be accustomed thus to quietness, is no small point gained to-
" wards fixing a habit of patience, and recollection, which seldom
" forsakes those who have been properly instructed in this entrance
" of the school of wisdom, during the residue of their days."

FOR

For the purpofe of acquiring this branch of education, children cannot affociate too early, nor too often with their parents, or with their fuperiors in age—rank—and wifdom.

12. The effects of Music upon the moral faculty, have been felt and recorded in every country. Hence we are able to difcover the virtues and vices of different nations, by their tunes, as certainly as by their laws. The effects of mufic, when fimply mechanical, upon the paffions, are powerful and extenfive. But it remains yet to determine the degrees of moral extafy, that may be produced by an attack upon the ear, the reafon, and the moral principle, at the fame time, by the combined powers of mufic and eloquence.

13. The Eloquence of the Pulpit is nearly allied to mufic in its effects upon the moral faculty. It is true, there can be no permanent change in the temper, and moral conduct of a man, that is not derived from the underftanding and the will; but we muft remember, that thefe two powers of the mind are moft affailable, when they are attacked through the avenue of the paffions; and thefe, we know, when agitated by the powers of eloquence, exert a mechanical action upon every power of the foul. Hence we find in every age and country, where chriftianity has been propagated, the moft accomplifhed orators have generally been the moft fuccefsful reformers of mankind. There muft be a defect of eloquence in a preacher, who with the refources for oratory, which are contained in the old and new teftaments, does not produce in every man who hears him, at leaft a temporary love of virtue. I grant that the eloquence of the pulpit alone, cannot change men into chriftians, but it certainly poffeffes the power of changing brutes

into men. Could the eloquence of the stage be properly directed, it is impossible to conceive the extent of its mechanical effects upon morals. The language and imagery of a Shakespear, upon moral and religious subjects, poured upon the passions and the senses, in all the beauty and variety of dramatic representation!——— Who could resist,—or describe their effects?

14. Odors of various kinds have been observed to act in the most sensible manner upon the moral faculty. Brydone tells us, upon the authority of a celebrated philosopher in Italy, that the peculiar wickedness of the people who live in the neighbourhood of Ætna and Vesuvius, is occasioned chiefly by the smell of the sulphur and of the hot exhalations which are constantly discharged from those volcanos. Agreeable odors, seldom fail to inspire serenity, and to compose the angry spirits—Hence the pleasure, and one of the advantages of a flower garden. The smoke of tobacco is likewise of a sedative nature, and tends not only to produce what is called a train in perception, but to hush the agitated passions into silence and order.—Hence the propriety of connecting the pipe or segar and the bottle together, in public company.

15. It is to be lamented, that no experiments have as yet been made, to determine the effects of all the different species of Airs, which chemistry has lately discovered, upon the moral faculty. I have authority, from actual experiments only, to declare, that DEPHLOGISTICATED AIR, when taken into the lungs, produces cheerfulness—gentleness—and serenity of mind.

16. What shall we say of the effects of Medicines upon the moral faculty?———That many substances in the materia medica act upon the intellects, is well known to physicians. Why should it be thought impossible for medicines, to act in like manner upon the moral faculty? May not the earth contain in its bowels, or upon its surface, antidotes to all our moral, as well as natural diseases?———Let those, who refuse to follow me in this conjecture, recollect, that moral evil was introduced into our minds—as well as natural evil into our bodies—by eating an apple.

Let it not be suspected from any thing that I have delivered, that I suppose the influence of physical causes upon the moral faculty, renders the agency of divine influence unnecessary to our moral happiness. I only maintain, that the operations of the divine government are carried on in the moral, as in the natural world,—by the instrumentality of second causes. I have only trodden in the footsteps of the inspired writers; for most of the physical causes I have enumerated, are connected with moral precepts, or have been used as the means of reformation from vice, in the old and new testaments. To the cases that have been mentioned I shall only add, that Nebuchadnezzar was cured of his pride, by means of solitude and a vegetable diet.———Saul was cured of his evil spirit, by means of David's harp—and St. Paul expressly says, " I " keep my body under, and bring it into subjection, lest that by any " means, when I have preached to others, I myself should be a cast " away." But I will go one step further, and add in favor of divine influence upon the moral principle, that in those extraordinary cases, where bad men are suddenly reformed, without the instrumentality of physical—moral—or rational causes, I believe

that

that the organization of those parts of the body, which form the link that binds it to the soul, undergoes a physical change*; and hence the expressions of a "new creature," which are made use of in the scriptures to denote this change, are proper in a literal, as well as a figurative sense. It is probably the beginning of that perfect renovation of the human body, which is predicted by St. Paul in the following words—" For our conversation is " in heaven,—from whence we look for the Saviour, who shall " change our VILE BODIES, that they may be fashioned according " to his own glorious body "

I CANNOT help remarking under this head, that if the conditions of those parts of the human body, which are connected with the soul, influence morals, the same reason may be given for a virtuous education, that has been admitted for teaching music and the pronunciation of foreign languages, in the early and yielding state of those organs, which form the voice and speech. Such is the effect of a moral education, that we often see its fruits in the advanced stages of life, after the religious principles which were connected with it, have been renounced. Just as we perceive the same care in a surgeon in his attendance upon his patients, after the sympathy which first produced this care, has ceased to operate upon his mind.— The boasted morality of the Deists, is I believe, in most cases, the offspring of habits, produced originally by the principles

---

* St. Paul was suddenly transformed from a persecutor, into a man of a gentle and amiable spirit. The manner in which this change was effected upon his mind, he tells us in the following words——" Neither circumcision availeth any thing, nor un- " circumcision, but the new creature.—From hence forth let no man trouble me; for " I bear in *my body*, the *marks* of our Lord Jesus." Galatians, VI. 15. 17.

ciples and precepts of chriſtianity.— Hence appears the wiſdom of " Solomon's advice—"Train up a child in the way he ſhould go, " and when he is old he will not"—I had almoſt ſaid,—he cannot "depart from it."

THUS have I enumerated the principal cauſes, which act mechanically upon morals. If, from the combined action of phyſical powers that are oppoſed to each other, the moral faculty ſhould become ſtationary, or if the virtue or vice produced by them, ſhould form a neutral quality, compoſed of both of them, I hope it will not call in queſtion the truth of our general propoſitions. I have only mentioned the effects of phyſical cauſes in a ſimple ſtate.

IT might help to enlarge our ideas upon this ſubject, to take notice of the influence of the different ſtages of ſociety—of agriculture, and commerce—of ſoil and ſituation—of the different degrees of cultivation of taſte, and of the intellectual powers— of the different forms of government—and laſtly of the different profeſſions and occupations of mankind, upon the moral faculty; but as theſe act indirectly only, and by the intervention of cauſes that are unconnected with matter, I conceive they are foreign to the buſineſs of the preſent enquiry. If they ſhould vary the action of the ſimple phyſical cauſes in any degree, I hope it will not call in queſtion the truth of our general propoſitions, any more than the compound action of phyſical powers, that are oppoſed to each other. There remain only a few more cauſes which are of a compound nature, but ſo nearly related to thoſe, which are purely

H mechanical

mechanical, that I shall beg leave to trespass upon your patience, by giving them a place in my oration.

The effects of Imitation—Habit—and Association upon morals, would furnish ample matter for investigation. Considering how much the shape, texture, and conditions of the human body, influence morals, I submit it to the consideration of the ingenious, whether in our endeavours to imitate moral examples, some advantage may not be derived, from our copying the features and external manners of the originals. What makes the success of this experiment probable is, that we generally find men, whose faces resemble each other, have the same manners and dispositions. I infer the possibility of success in an attempt to imitate originals in the manner that has been mentioned, from the facility with which domestics acquire a resemblance to their masters and mistresses, not only in manners, but in countenance, in those cases where they are tied to them, by respect, and affection.—Husbands and wives also, where they possess the same species of face, under circumstances of mutual attachment, often acquire a resemblance to each other.

From the general detestation in which hypocrisy is held both by good and bad men, the mechanical effects of Habit upon virtue, have not been sufficiently explored. There are, I am persuaded, many instances, where virtues have been assumed by accident, or necessity, which have become real from habit, and afterwards derived their nourishment from the heart. Hence the wisdom of Hamlet's advice to his mother———

" Assume a virtue; if you have it not,
" That monster, custom, who all sense doth eat,

" Of

" Of habits evil, is angel, yet in this,
" That to the use of actions fair and good,
" He likewise gives a frock or livery,
" That aptly is put on——Refrain to-night,
" And that shall lend a kind of easiness,
" To the next abstinence; the next more easy,
" For use can almost change the stamp of nature,
" And master even the devil, or throw him out,
" With wonderous potency."

THE influence of ASSOCIATION upon morals, opens an ample field for enquiry. It is from this principle, that we explain the reformation from theft and drunkenness in servants which we sometimes see produced by a draught of spirits in which tartar emetic had been secretly dissolved. The recollection of the pain and sickness excited by the emetic, naturally associates itself with the spirits, so as to render them both equally the objects of aversion. It is by calling in this principle only, that we can account for the conduct of Moses, in grinding the golden calf into a powder, and afterwards dissolving it (probably by means of hepar sulphuris) in water, and compelling the children of Israel to drink of it, as a punishment for their idolatry. This mixture is bitter and nauseating in the highest degree. It could not be remembered therefore, by them, without being associated with an equal abhorrence of their folly and wickedness. The benefit of corporal punishments, when they are of a short duration, depends in part upon their being connected by time and place, with the crimes for which they are inflicted. Quick as the thunder follows the lightning, if it were possible, should punishments follow crimes, and the advantage of

association

affociation would be more certain, if the fpot where they were committed, were made the theatre of their expiation. It is from the effects of this affociation, probably, that the change of place and company produced by exile and tranfportation, has fo often reclaimed bad men, after moral—rational—and phyfical means of reformation had been ufed to no purpofe.

As SENSIBILITY is the avenue to the moral faculty, every thing which tends to diminifh it, tends alfo, to injure morals.——The Romans owed much of their corruption to the fights of the contefts of their gladiators, and of criminals, with wild beafts. For thefe reafons, executions fhould never be public. Indeed, I believe there are few public punifhments of any kind, that do not harden the hearts of fpectators, and thereby leffen the natural horror which all crimes at firft excite in the human mind.

CRUELTY to brute animals is another means of deftroying moral fenfibility. The ferocity of favages has been afcribed in part to their peculiar mode of fubfiftence. Mr. Hogarth points out in his ingenious prints, the connection between cruelty to brute animals in youth, and murder in manhood. The Emperor Domitian prepared his mind by the amufement of killing flies, for all thofe bloody crimes which afterwards difgraced his reign. I am fo perfectly fatisfied of the truth of a connection between morals, and humanity to brutes, that I fhall find it difficult to reftrain my idolatry for that legiflature, that fhall firft eftablifh a fyftem of laws, to defend them from outrage and oppreffion.

In order to preserve the vigor of the moral faculty, it is of the utmost consequence to keep young people as ignorant as possible of those crimes, that are generally thought most disgraceful to human nature. Suicide, I believe, is often propagated by means of newspapers. For this reason, I should be glad to see the proceedings of our courts kept from the public eye, when they expose, or punish monstrous vices.

The last mechanical method of promoting morality that I shall mention, is to keep sensibility alive, by a familiarity with scenes of distress from poverty and disease. Compassion never awakens in the human bosom, without being accompanied with a train of sister virtues—hence the wise man justly remarks, that " By the sad-" ness of the countenance, the heart is made better."

A late French writer in his prediction of events that are to happen in the year 4000, says " That mankind in that æra shall " be so far improved by religion and government, that the sick " and the dying, shall no longer be thrown together with the " dead, into splendid houses, but shall be relieved and protected in " a connection with their families and society." For the honor of humanity, an institution * destined for that distant period, has lately been founded in this city, that shall perpetuate the year 1786 in the history of Pennsylvania. Here the feeling heart—the tearful eye—and the charitable hand, may always be connected together, and the flame of sympathy, instead of being extinguished in taxes, or expiring in a solitary blaze by a single contribution, may be kept alive,

* A public dispensary.

alive, by conſtant exerciſe. There is a neceſſary connection between animal ſympathy and morals. The prieſt and the levite, in the new teſtament, would probably have relieved the poor man who fell among thieves, had accident brought them near enough to examine his wounds. The unfortunate Mrs. Bellamy was reſcued from the dreadful purpoſe of drowning herſelf, by nothing but the diſtreſs of a child, rending the air with its cries for bread. It is probably owing in ſome meaſure to the connection between morals and ſympathy, that the fair ſex in every age, and country, have been more diſtinguiſhed for virtue, than men—for who ever heard of a woman, devoid of humanity?———

Lastly, Attraction, Composition, and Decomposition, belong to the paſſions as well as to matter. Vices of the ſame ſpecies attract each other with the moſt force—hence the bad conſequences of crouding young men (whoſe propenſities are generally the ſame) under one roof, in our modern plans of education. The effects of compoſition and decompoſition upon vices, appear in the meanneſs of the ſchool boy, being often cured by the prodigality of a military life, and by the precipitation of avarice, which is often produced by ambition and love.

If phyſical cauſes influence morals in the manner we have deſcribed, may they not alſo influence religious principles and opinions?—I anſwer in the affirmative; and I have authority, from the records of phyſic, as well as from my own obſervations, to declare, that religious melancholy and madneſs, in all their variety of ſpecies, yield with more facility to medicine, than ſimply to polemical diſcourſes, or to caſuiſtical advice.— But this ſubject is foreign to the buſineſs of the preſent enquiry. From

[35]

From a review of our subject, we are led to contemplate with admiration, the curious structure of the human mind. How distinct are the number, and yet how united! How subordinate, and yet how coequal are all its powers! How wonderful is the action of the soul upon the body!—Of the body upon the soul!—And of the divine spirit upon both! What a mystery is the mind of man to itself!———O! nature!——Or to speak more properly,——O! thou, God of Nature!———In vain do we attempt to scan thy immensity, or to comprehend thy various modes of existence, when a single particle of light issued from thyself, and kindled into intelligence in the bosom of man, thus dazzles and confounds our understandings!———

The extent of the moral powers and habits in man is unknown. It is not improbable, but the human mind contains principles of virtue, which have never yet been excited into action. We behold with surprise the versatility of the human body, in the exploits of tumblers and ropedancers. Even the agility of a wild beast has been demonstrated in a girl in France, and an amphibious nature has been discovered in the human species, in a young man in Spain. We listen with astonishment to the accounts of the *memories* of Mithridates, Cyrus, and Servin.—We feel a veneration bordering upon divine homage, in contemplating the stupendous *understandings* of Lord Verulam and Sir Isaac Newton; and our eyes grow dim, in attempting to pursue Shakespear and Milton in their immeasurable flights of *imagination*.—And if the history of mankind does not furnish similar instances of the versatility and perfection of our species in virtue, it is, because the moral faculty has been the subject of less culture and fewer experiments than the body, and the
intellectual

intellectual powers of the mind. From what has been said, the reason of this is obvious. Hitherto the cultivation of the moral faculty has been the business of parents, schoolmasters and divines.* But if the principles, we have laid down, be just, the improvement and extension of this principle should be equally the business of the legislator—the natural philosopher—and the physician; and a physical regimen should as necessarily accompany a moral precept, as directions with respect to air—exercise—and diet, generally accompany prescriptions for the consumption, and the gout. To encourage us to undertake experiments for the improvement of morals, let us recollect the success of philosophy in lessening the number, and mitigating the violence of incurable diseases. The intermitting fever, which proved fatal to two of the monarchs of Britain, is now under absolute subjection to medicine. Continual fevers are much less fatal than formerly. The smallpox is disarmed of its mortality by inoculation, and even the tetanus and the cancer have lately received a check in their ravages upon mankind. But medicine has done more—It has penetrated the deep and gloomy abyss of death, and acquired fresh honors in his cold embraces.——Witness the many hundred people, who have lately been brought back to life, by the successful efforts of the humane societies, which are now established in many parts of Europe, and in some parts of America.

Should

* The people commonly called Quakers and the Methodists, make use of the greatest number of physical remedies in their religious and moral discipline, of any sects of christians ——and hence we find them every where distinguished for their morals. There are several excellent *physical* institutions in other churches; and if they do not produce the same moral effects, that we observe from physical institutions among those two modern sects, it must be ascribed to their being more neglected by the members of those churches.

Should the same industry and ingenuity, which have produced these triumphs of medicine over diseases and death, be applied to the moral science, it is highly probable, that most of those baneful vices, which deform the human breast and convulse the nations of the earth, might be banished from the world. I am not so sanguine as to suppose, that it is possible for man to acquire so much perfection from science, religion, liberty and good government, as to cease to be mortal; but I am fully persuaded, that from the combined action of causes, which operate at once upon the reason, the moral faculty, the passions, the senses, the brain, the nerves, the blood and the heart, it is possible to produce such a change in the moral character of man, as shall raise him to a resemblance of angels—nay more, to the likeness of GOD himself.———The State of Pennsylvania still deplores the loss of a man, in whom not only reason and revelation, but many of the physical causes that have been enumerated, concurred to produce such attainments in moral excellency, as have seldom appeared in a human being. This amiable citizen, considered his fellow creature, man, as God's extract, from his own works; and whether this image of himself, was cut out from ebony or copper—whether he spoke his own, or a foreign language—or whether he worshiped his Maker with ceremonies, or without them, he still considered him as a brother, and equally the object of his benevolence. Poets and historians, who are to live hereafter, to you I commit his panegyric; and when you hear of a law for abolishing slavery in each of the American States, such as was passed in Pennsylvania, in the year 1780—when you hear of the kings and queens of Europe, publishing edicts for abolishing the trade in human souls—and lastly, when you hear of schools and churches, with all the arts of civilized life, being established among the nations of Africa, then remember and record, that this revolution in favor of human happiness, was the effect of the labors—the publications—the private letters—and the prayers of ANTHONY BENEZET.*

I RETURN from this digression, to address myself in a particular manner to you, VENERABLE SAGES, and FELLOW CITIZENS in the REPUBLIC of LETTERS.— The influence of philosophy, we have been told, has already been felt in courts. To increase, and complete this influence, there is nothing more necessary, than for the numerous literary societies in Europe and America, to add the SCIENCE of MORALS to their experiments and enquiries. The godlike scheme of Henry the IV. of France, and of the illustrious Queen Elizabeth of England, for establishing a perpetual peace in Europe, may be accomplished without a system of jurisprudence, by a confederation of learned men, and learned societies. It is in their power, by multiplying the objects of human reason, to bring the monarchs and

* This worthy man was descended from an ancient and honorable family that flourished in the court of Lewis the XIV. With liberal prospects in life, he early devoted himself to teaching an English school; in which, for industry, capacity, and attention to the morals and principles of the youth committed to his care, he was without an equal. He published many excellent tracts against the African trade, against war, and the use of spirituous liquors, and one in favor of civilising and christianising the Indians. He wrote to the queen of Great-Britain, and the queen of Portugal, to use their influence in their respective courts to abolish the African trade. He also wrote an affectionate letter to the king of Prussia, to dissuade him from making war. The history of his life affords a remarkable instance how much it is possible for an individual to accomplish in the world; and that the most humble stations do not preclude good men from the most extensive usefulness. He bequeathed his estate (after the death of his widow) to the support of a school for the education of negro children, which he had founded and taught for several years before he died. He departed this life in May 1784, in the 71st year of his age, in the meridian of his usefulness, universally lamented by persons of all ranks and denominations.

and rulers of the world, under their subjection, and thereby to extirpate war—slavery—and capital punishments, from the list of human evils. Let it not be suspected that I detract by this declaration, from the honor of the christian religion. It is true—christianity was propagated without the aid of human learning; but this was one of those miracles, which was necessary to establish it, and which, by repetition, would cease to be a miracle. They misrepresent the christian religion, who suppose it to be wholly an internal revelation, and addressed only to the moral powers of the mind. The truths of christianity afford the greatest scope for the human understanding, and they will become intelligible to us, only in proportion as the human genius is stretched by means of philosophy, to its utmost dimensions. Errors may be opposed to errors; but truths, upon all subjects, mutually support each other. And perhaps one reason, why some parts of the christian revelation are still involved in obscurity, may be occasioned by our imperfect knowledge of the phænomena, and laws of nature. The truths of philosophy and christianity, dwell alike in the mind of the Deity, and reason and religion are equally the offspring of his goodness. They must, therefore, stand and fall together. By reason, in the present instance, I mean the power of judging of truth, as well as the power of comprehending it. Happy æra!——When the divine and the philosopher shall embrace each other, and unite their labors, for the reformation and happiness of mankind!———

Illustrious Councillors and Senators of Pennsylvania!*
I anticipate your candid reception of this feeble effort to encrease the
quantity

* His excellency the president, and supreme executive council, and the members of the general assembly of Pennsylvania, attended the delivery of the oration, in the hall of the university, by invitation from the philosophical society.

quantity of virtue in our republic. It is not my bufinefs to remind you of the immenfe refources for greatnefs, which nature and Providence have beftowed upon our ftate. Every advantage which France has derived from being placed in the centre of Europe, and which Britain has derived from her mixture of nations, Pennfylvania has opened to her. But my bufinefs at prefent, is to fuggeft the means of promoting the happinefs, not the greatnefs of the ftate. For this purpofe, it is abfolutely neceffary that our government, which unites into one all the minds of the ftate, fhould poffefs, in an eminent degree, not only the underftanding, the paffions, and the will, but above all, the moral faculty, and the confcience of an individual.—Nothing can be politically right, that is morally wrong; and no neceffity can ever fanctify a law, that is contrary to equity. VIRTUE is the living principle of a republic. To promote this, laws for the fuppreffion of vice and immorality will be as ineffectual, as the encreafe and enlargement of gaols.—— There is but one method of preventing crimes, and of rendering a republican form of government durable, and that is by diffeminating the feeds of virtue and knowledge through every part of the ftate, by means of proper modes and places of education, and this can be done effectually only, by the interference and aid of the legiflature. I am fo deeply impreffed with the truth of this opinion, that were this evening to be the laft of my life, I would not only fay to the afylum of my anceftors, and my beloved native country, with the patriot of Venice, " Efto perpetua,"—But I would add, as the laft proof of my gratitude and affection for her, my parting advice to the guardians of her liberties, " To eftablifh and fupport PUBLIC SCHOOLS in " every part of the ftate."

SIX INTRODUCTORY LECTURES,

TO

COURSES OF LECTURES,

UPON THE

INSTITUTES AND PRACTICE

OF

MEDICINE,

DELIVERED IN THE

UNIVERSITY OF PENNSYLVANIA.

BY BENJAMIN RUSH, M. D.

PROFESSOR OF MEDICINE IN THE SAID UNIVERSITY.

PHILADELPHIA:

PUBLISHED BY JOHN CONRAD, & CO. NO. 30, CHESNUT-STREET, PHILADELPHIA; M. & J. CONRAD, & CO. NO. 144, MARKET-STREET, BALTIMORE; AND RAPIN, CONRAD, & CO. WASHINGTON CITY:

H. MAXWELL, PRINTER.

1801.

LECTURE IV.

ON THE

INFLUENCE OF PHYSICAL CAUSES

IN PROMOTING AN

INCREASE OF THE STRENGTH

AND ACTIVITY OF THE

INTELLECTUAL FACULTIES OF MAN.

DELIVERED NOVEMBER 18th, 1799.

GENTLEMEN,

OUR introductory lecture this year shall consist of a few remarks upon the influence of physical causes, in promoting an increase of the strength and activity of the intellectual faculties of man.

This subject is highly interesting to gentlemen of all professions, but it is peculiarly so to physicians, whose studies and duties require the utmost extent and force, of all the faculties of the mind.

I include in them, upon the present occasion, the understanding, the memory, and the imagination. The influence of physical causes upon the moral faculties of the mind, has been considered in another place.

I pass by the knotty question of the specific nature of the mind. It will be sufficient for the purposes of our present inquiry, to believe, that all its operations are the effects of bodily impressions. This belief accords with the old and long received axiom of the schools....viz. " Nihil est in intellectu, quod non prius fuit in sensu," that is, in other words, the understanding contains no knowledge of any kind, but what was conveyed to it through the avenues of the senses.

In this attempt to show the influence of physical causes, upon the intellectual faculties, I shall confine myself only to those agents which increase the quantity of mind. The causes which lessen it, belong to pathology, and will be enumerated in the second part of the institutes of medicine.

Before I enter upon our subject, I shall remark further, that it is a practical one. Our lecture of course will consist chiefly of facts, which I shall enumerate in an order that will render them intelligible to the youngest student of medicine.

I shall begin by taking notice of the relation of the strength, and activity of the intellectual faculties

1st. To aliment. Abstinence imparts to the memory and understanding, a high degree of vigour. The aid which those two faculties, when thus excited, afford to devotion, has rendered fasting common in most of the religions of the world. Travels and voyages furnish many instances of the wonderful fertility of the mind in persons who are in danger of perishing from famine. Gamesters become acute, by abstaining from food for two days before they sit down to a card table. Such are the beneficial effects of inanition upon the mind, that Carneades, a noted philosopher in Greece, always made it a practice to increase it by taking a purge of Hellebore, before he disputed with Chrysippus a distinguished philosopher of the sect of stoics.

Temperance, which consists in eating less than the appetite calls for, has a friendly influence upon the operations of the mind. Sir Isaac Newton lived upon nothing but vegetables, while he was employed in composing his famous treatise upon Opticks. Our illustrious countryman, Mr. Edwards, tells us in his diary, that he always studied to most advantage, after a temperate meal. A hundred other instances of a similar nature might be mentioned. Even whole nations bear testimony to the good effects of simple diet upon the intellectual faculties. A broth of a black colour was supposed to have given the Spartans their mental pre-eminence over all their neighbours, and the barley broth of Scotland, probably contributes no small share to form the reputation which the people of that country have acquired for genius and knowledge, in every part of the world.

However great the benefits and praise of abstinence and temperance may be, I am obliged to add, there are a few instances to be met with, in which a full diet, consisting of gross animal food, has produced great activity of intellect. Dr. Zimmerman informs us that Frederick II. king of Prussia, was a great eater, and many private accounts assure us, that some of the most distinguished literary characters of the present day are devoted to the pleasures of the table. As far as I have been able to learn, most of these acute and ingenious gluttons are, or have been subject to great depression of spirits. Large meals become of course necessary to elevate their minds to the ordinary grade at which the faculties act with vigour. The effects of a full diet upon most persons, is the reverse of what has been mentioned. It generally weakens the intellectual faculties, and instances are not wanting, of its having produced a total extinction of them in the most deplorable fatuity.

2d. The use of certain drinks is connected with vigour, and celerity in the operations of the mind. The intellects of Demosthenes in ancient, and of Dr. Haller in modern times, were kept in a state of regular excitement, by their drinking nothing but water. Wine, when taken in moderation, produces wit and humour in company. It multiplies images in the imagination of the poet, and sometimes creates new combinations of ideas in the understanding of the philosopher. Ardent spirits have sometimes had the same effects. Coffee and tea excite the understanding in the most agreeable manner. The former was the mental stimulus of Voltaire. The latter was used so constantly for the same purpose by the celebrated Dr. Johnson, that the water in his tea-kettle, it is said, was seldom cold. Happily for the interests of science and literature, those two pleasant infusions have become the cordials of studious men in many parts of the world, and thereby rescued them from the baneful effects of intoxicating liquors.

3d. Opium exerts a friendly and agreeable influence upon the intellects. The late Mr. John Hunter never rose to deliver a lecture, without previously exciting his faculties by means of a dose of laudanum. Dr. Johnson, an ingenious physician, who visited our city in 1794, informed me, that during a residence of fourteen years in India, he had learned to drink, as a common beverage, an emulsion made of poppies, which he found to have a powerful effect in invigorating the faculties of his mind.

4th. Tobacco acts upon the understanding by its stimulus predominating over all other impressions, which, by distracting sensations, prevent the accumulation of that degree of excitement in the brain, that is favourable to a vigorous and connected train of thought. The well-known Hobbes always sat in his study inveloped in the smoke of ten or twelve pipes of tobacco. An eminent dissenting clergyman in England composed a system of divinity, with streams of saliva impregnated with tobacco, issuing from his mouth; and Frederick II, king of Prussia, resorted to a profuse use of snuff, to elevate his mind above the pressure of the difficulties and dangers of his last seven years' war.

Where the use of this weed in any way has been habitual, we sometimes see the want of it followed by great languor in the intellectual faculties. This languor has been seen to yield, in an instant, to a pinch of snuff, or a segar. Let us not suppose, from these facts, that tobacco has a necessary and original influence in producing force or connection in the operations of the mind. It acts in this way, only upon persons who are accustomed to it. Thus, garlic imparts health to some people, but it is only to those who have been in the habit of living upon that loathsome vegetable. In persons who are unaccustomed to it, it excites sickness at stomach, and many other distressing commotions in the body.

5th. Different positions of the body, and different exercises, have a sensible influence upon the intellectual faculties. Descartes composed his works in bed. Mr. Brindley found a recumbent posture most favourable to the exertions of his genius, and hence we are told, he sometimes laid in bed for three days, when he was obliged to plan a new and difficult piece of machinery. Rousseau tells us in his Confessions, that most of his original thoughts were suggested to him in bed. I have known many other instances, in which, this posture of the body has proved favourable to the production of new, and the revival of old ideas. It is much assisted by the silence and darkness of night, and by the empty state of the stomach in the morning.

In some persons the intellects are excited by a *standing* position. Col. Charles Townshend, (so much admired in the British House of Commons, about 30 years ago) was eloquent, only when he stood upon his feet, and so sensible was he of it, that he would often rise from his seat at a convivial table, in order to give more force and charms to his conversation. The late judge Wilson, whose abilities and knowledge, will never be forgotten by the friends of the revolution, and government of the United States, has assured me, that his ideas always flowed most easily when he was upon his feet. This was so much the case, that I have repeatedly observed him when closely pushed in an argument, or deeply engaged in conversation, to rise from his chair in company, and occupy a fixed position in a corner of a room. The late sir Joshua Reynolds always painted in a standing posture. I need hardly add, that his pencil has given celebrity to the country in which he lived. WALKING assists the operations of the intellectual faculties in an eminent degree. A sect of philosophers who were remarkable for studying and teaching, while they were employed in this exercise, obtained from thence the name of Peripatetics. Rousseau derived many of his new ideas, he tells us, from walking amidst rocks and mountains. RIDING, whether on horseback, or a carriage, favours thought, and hence the practice of some travellers to carry common place books with them, to record their original thoughts the moment they occur, lest, in their number and variety, they should be lost before they reached the end of their excursions. Many of the elegant ideas of Mr. Pope, we are told, were excited in his brain by riding a trotting horse. The late Mr. Edwards found this mode of exercise to pour such a stream of new ideas into his mind, that in visiting his parishioners, he often retired from the road into the woods, and dismounted his horse, in order that he might, without interruption, empty the overflowings of his genius into his pocket memorandum book.

6th. Loose dresses contribute to the easy and vigorous exercise of the faculties of the mind. This remark is so obvious, and so generally known, that we find studious men are always painted in gowns, when they are seated in their libraries. Sometimes an open collar, and loose shoes and stockings, form a part of their picture. It is from the habits of mental ease and vigour which this careless form of dress creates, that learned men have often become contemptible for their slovenly appearance, when they mix with the world.

7th. Weakness, disease, and pain, have, in many instances, given a preternatural excitement to the human intellects. Cicero, Erasmus, Pascal, and Boilieu, were all known to their contemporaries, as much by the feebleness of their constitutions, as by the strength of their minds. The great mental vigour, which has been observed in persons who are hump-backed, of which, the celebrated Roman orator Galba, and Mr. Pope, furnished memorable instances, is probably occasioned by the bodily weakness that is connected with deformity. But the effects of disease, whether occasional or chronic, in an èvolving mind, are still more remarkable. How often do we hear our patients discover, upon a sick or death-bed, marks of reflection, and even eloquence, to which they were strangers when they were in health! It has been remarked, that abortive and sickly children make sensible men and women*. Disease, in these cases, acts in various ways. It imposes a restraint upon their appetites, it confines them to the company of their parents, and of persons who are capable of improving them, and it certainly keeps up an action in the brain, in common with other parts of the body, which tends to impart vigour to the intellectual faculties.

But further. There are several well-attested instances upon record, of persons speaking long-forgotten languages in the delirium of a fever, and one, related by Dr. Frank, of a man, who spoke a language in a diseased state of his brain, which he

---

* The first lord Lyttelton, and the late Mrs. Elizabeth Ferguson of Pennsylvania, were both seven months' children. The writings of the former will always remain as evidences of a great and vigorous understanding. The latter, for more than forty years, was admired by both sexes for her uncommon talents. What Dr. Johnson says of Mr. Burke, may be said of her, with a small addition. " Her conversa- " tion," and letters, " were a stream of mind."

had never learned. If this be true, he must have heard the words of it, without understanding their meaning, for it is impossible to conceive of the knowledge of even a single sound existing in the mind, unless it had been previously conveyed there through the medium of the ears.

In support of the influence of diseases in exciting the faculties of the mind, let us attend to the phenomena of diseases, which are produced by a morbid state of the brain. The intellects act here without order, but they act with uncommon celerity and force. Of this, every man must be convinced, who has paid the least attention to those operations in his own mind. The business of a day is often transacted in a dream, in the course of a single minute, and the perception of supposed impressions upon the imagination, are far more vivid than in the waking state. Even madness discovers the connection between morbid excitement in the body, and an increase of vigour and activity in certain intellectual operations. Who has not heard preternatural and brilliant effusions of eloquence, and wit in the cell of an hospital? The disease, in this instance, resembles an earthquake, which, in rending the ground, now and then throws upon its surface, with many offensive matters, certain precious fossils, which surprise and delight us by their novelty or splendour.

The effects of pain, in generating new ideas, or exciting old ones in a rapid succession, have been taken notice of in my account of the influence of physical causes upon the moral faculty. To the facts I have there mentioned, I shall add two more. The famous pedestrian traveller, Mr. Stewart, informed me, that he had seen torture produce short intervals of reason in some idiots in Italy. I have known the pain of a large abscess upon the back, produce the same effect upon a man, who had been confined for madness, which ended in fatuity, above twenty years in the Pennsylvania hospital.

8th. Moderate sleep preserves and increases the energy of the mind. It is always in excess, when it exceeds the third part of an astronomical day. Much less has been found sufficient for health and comfort, in the most distinguished persons, who have lived in the republic of science and letters. Mr. John Westley, who died in the eighty-sixth year of his age, with all his faculties in their full vigour, seldom slept more than four hours in the four and twenty. The morning is more favourable to the rapid and easy exercises of the mind, than any other part of the day. The results of midnight-studies are said, " to smell of the lamp," because they generally discover marks of drowsiness or labour.

9th. Certain sounds have the power of exciting the faculties of the mind, into preternatural action. The effects of music upon them is well-known. Poets and mathematicians have, in many instances, found their talents for invention assisted by a tune upon a violin or a german flute.

10th. A certain temperature of the air, is favourable to the vigorous operation of the faculties of the mind. This temperature is different in different people. It has generally that degree of heat in it, which is not accompanied with any sensation. Cold or heat, when perceptible, distract the excitement of the brain, and thereby interrupt thought. It is only when the exercises of the mind are conducted with uncommon vigour, that we lose our perceptions of the impressions of heat and cold. The suspension of those exercises, and even the least relaxation of them, is immediately followed by a sense of profuse and distressing sweats in summer, or of a painful coldness in the hands and feet in winter. The genius of Milton poured forth its sublime and harmonious ideas, only in the spring and autumn. I have never heard of but one person, whose mental faculties were improved by cold. It was a student of mathematics, who used to remove the embarrassment produced by a difficult problem, by taking off his wig, and exposing his bare head to the north-west wind, in the middle of winter.

11th. Rural and mountainous situations have an influence in exciting the intellects into vigorous action. The poets of every age and country have uniformly derived the principal stimulus to their minds from country scenes. The Eclogues of Virgil, the Windsor Forest of Pope, the Seasons of Thompson, and the Poems of Ossian, all bear witness to the truth of this remark. The effects of these rural scenes are much increased by their novelty. It is from the variety and constant succession of *new* objects, both natural and artificial, acting upon the mind, that young men sometimes acquire, not only knowledge, but intellect by visiting foreign countries. It is from the same cause probably, that boys who appear to be deficient in capacity, learn well when sent from home to a city, or country school.

12th. Great height has produced, in several instances, uncommon activity in the intellectual faculties. An ingenious foreigner lately informed me, that he had once conversed with a man who had spent several hours upon the summit of the steeple at Strasburg, who told him that his mind, while there, was overwhelmed by the variety and originality of his thoughts. We have heard much of the pleasure which many persons have felt in traversing the upper regions of the air in a balloon. It is to be lamented that they have neglected to record, at the same time, the influence of that new situation, upon the operations of their minds.*

---

* The Abbe Spallanzani describes the state of his mind, upon the summit of mount Ætna, in the following words; " Seated in the midst of this theatre of the wonders of nature, I felt an indescribable pleasure from the multiplicity, and beauty of the objects I surveyed, and a kind of internal satisfaction and exultation of heart. The sun was advancing to the meridian unobscured by the smallest cloud, and Reaumur's thermometer stood at the tenth degree above the freezing point. I was therefore in that temperature which is most friendly to man, and the refined air I breathed, (as if it had been entirely vital) communicated a vigour and agility to my limbs, and a *life* and *activity* to my ideas which appeared to be of a celestial nature." Travels into the two Sicilies. vol. i. p. 285.

In his account of the islands of Felicuda and Alicuda, he adds further; " As to the content and tranquillity of these islanders, and the affection they bear their native country, I do not think I should greatly err, were I to ascribe it to the happy temperature of the climate, and

13th. The great variety and constant succession of new impressions, which occur in large cities, from business, news, company, theatres, shews, controversies and casualties, have a powerful effect in increasing, the strength and activity of the intellects. London and Paris have been for many centuries the hot-beds of men who have adorned, and enlightened the British and French nations. Such is the combined force of mental impressions in those great capitals, that they impart rapidity to the movements of the body, and particularly to the organs of speech. This is so much the case, that the citizens of London and Paris are often known by their walking, and speaking quicker than the inhabitants of villages, and country places.

14th. Silence and solitude have always been considered as favourable to intellectual attainments. It was to avoid noise, that the philosophers of Greece retired to groves, and sequestered

---

the quality of the air, which when pure, so much contributes to maintain in us the proper harmony between the solids and fluids, or the state of perfect health. A proof of this, I experienced in myself. Notwithstanding the continual and great fatigues I underwent in my excursions among those rocks, and notwithstanding my advanced age, I felt in myself an energy of body, an *agility* and *liveliness* of mind, and an animation of my whole frame, which I had experienced no where else, except on the summit of mount Ætna. In countries infested with impure air and thick vapours, I have never been able to apply myself to my favourite studies immediately after dinner, but under this sky, which is so rarely overclouded with vapours, I could write on the spot at any time, a part of those observations I am now about to present to the public. Vol. iv. p. 149, 150.

places, impenetrable to distracting sounds of all kinds. The influence of solitude upon the understanding, has been ably pointed out by Dr. Zimmerman. To be useful, silence and solitude should be temporary, and always alternated with company.

14th. I hinted formerly at the beneficial effects of darkness upon the mind. Corneille shut his windows, and created an artificial darkness when he composed his plays. Mr. Woodfall always sat with his eyes closed, when he filled his memory with the speeches of the celebrated speakers in the British house of Commons, in order that he might copy, and print them afterwards in his news-paper. It was to obtain the utmost advantages from the absence of all the distracting objects which are obtruded by the light of the sun, that the famous council of Areopagus in Athens held all their sessions at night, and in the open air. The effects of perpetual darkness upon the mind in blind people are well known. Homer and Milton probably owed much of the vigour and extent of all their intellectual faculties, to the loss of their sight.

From a review of all the facts that have been mentioned, it is obvious, there is the same variety in the texture of the minds, that there is in the bodies of men. It would seem likewise, as if there was a certain point at which impressions produced the greatest vigour and celerity in the operations of the intellectual faculties. This point is influenced by the previous state of the brain with respect to elevation and depression. The impressions might have been divided into stimulating and sedative, were it not for the variety we observe in their effects, according to the different state of the brain in different people, and in the same people, at different times.

Having enumerated briefly all the physical causes which act obviously upon the mind in enlarging its faculties, I shall proceed next to mention a few more, which, though not admitted to be physical, act in the same way, by exciting, multiplying, and modifying motions in the brain, and thereby producing more vigorous emissions of thought.

1. There are certain studies which are calculated to increase the strength of the intellectual faculties in early life. They are, first, *natural history*. This science is strongly recommended to our notice and attention, by its having been the first study of the father of mankind, in the garden of Eden. It furnishes the raw materials of knowledge upon all subjects. By the fermentation they excite in the mind, they prepare it for embracing with facility the principles of general science.

2d. The amusements *of Checkers, Chess, and Riddles*, are calculated to impart strength to the minds of children, after they pass the seventh or eighth year of their lives.

3d. The study of *arithmetic and the mathematicks* have long been celebrated for their efficacy in awaking, strengthening, and arranging the thinking faculties. Where there is an inaptitude to them, they have sometimes been known to have a contrary effect. In no instance should they be obtruded upon young people, where they discover an inability to acquire them with facility or pleasure.

We sometimes meet with children who astonish us with the rapidity of their attainments in every kind of knowledge. These children are generally destined by superstitious people, not to " scratch a grey head." Many of them die prematurely, from the disproportion between the exercises of their minds, and the strength of their bodies, while those who survive these early achievements of genius, become sickly; or weaken their intellects before they attain to maturity. To prevent these consequences of premature vigour in their faculties, they should be seduced from study, by teaching them useful or ornamental *bodily* exercises. Rousseau, though often erroneous and paradoxical in his system of education, is just in saying, the exercises of the body should always precede those of the mind. I never can forget the pleasure with which I saw, for the first time, this excellent remark exemplified at the house of a gentleman in the neighbourhood of Edinburgh, who introduced one of his daughters, then about five years old, with a little spinning-wheel, at which she worked with great dexterity, singing at the same time a well known song, suited to her employment, to the great delight of a large and respectable company. The celebrated **David Hume**, Dr. Blacklock, and James Boswell composed a part of the guests at this agreeable entertainment.

2. Changing the objects of study, has a considerable influence in begetting strength and activity in the intellectual faculties. The new objects of study, act according to their nature, either as a fresh stimulus to the brain, or by producing a moderate relaxation in such parts of it as have been unduly exercised. The late lord Chatham made it a practice to excite his genius by reading a few pages of Dr. Barrow's theological works, before he took a part in the debates of the British House of Commons. The late Dr. Finley, frequently read a portion of Mr. Howe's meditations for the same purpose, when he preached without notes. Rousseau reduced the extravagant tone of his mind, by descending to light studies. Mr. M'Laurin relieved himself from the fatigue induced by his mathematical researches, by reading novels. Writing a letter, or reading a newspaper, has in some instances enabled persons to solve problems, which before eluded the utmost exertions of their powers.

3. The exercises of the faculties in *composing*, whether in prose or poetry, has a wonderful effect in strengthening and facilitating their operations. It is for this reason, that the composition of letters, declamations, disputes, and orations form an essential part of education, in all well-conducted

seminaries of learning. In attending public instruction, young men are *taught* by their masters, but in committing their thoughts to paper, they *teach* themselves. " The man," says Dr. Clark, " who wishes to become eminent in any profes" sion, must *read* much, *think* much, and *write* " much." The last of these exercises of the mind is indispensably necessary to give the highest vigour to a mind of which it is capable. Dr. Priestley has made it a constant practice to write upon every subject which he wished to understand perfectly, and to this thirst for extensive and accurate knowledge, may be ascribed, in part, his numerous publications. Even wit is evolved by means of the ink-stand. Dr. Arbuthnot, the friend of Swift, never said a witty thing in company, but his miscellaneous writings shew, that he possessed that talent in an eminent degree. The wit and satire of Peter Pindar flow likewise only upon paper. In conversation, it is said, he is not distinguished by them, from other men.

It has been remarked, that our dreams are most connected, when we imagine ourselves to be engaged in conversation. Speaking arrests the velocity of our thoughts, and gives them some degree of order. Composing acts in like manner, but with a greater effect in retarding the rapid succession and flight of our ideas. It is for this reason, that we often observe great and original thoughts evolved in a letter, by men, who are dull in conversation, and devoid of genius in the common business of their lives. Dr. Franklin was so sensible of the strength and correctness the mind derived from a slower current of ideas in writing, than in barely thinking; that he never undertook any important enterprise, without first committing to paper all the arguments for and against it, and afterwards placing them before his eyes, while he deliberated and decided upon it.

As the faculties have a reciprocal action upon each other, they should be all exercised together, or in a close succession. The memory should constantly be employed in administering materials for the understanding to act upon, and the imagination should occasionally be stimulated to furnish its images to both, by a recurrence to the poets. A page of Milton, or Young, or a line in Shakspeare, is, to a mind rendered languid by intellectual pursuits, like wine to the body, when debilitated by exercise or labour.

4. The passions, when excited, have a considerable influence upon the intellectual faculties. Lord Kaimes says, " he has seldom known a man " of great genius, who was not more or less under " the dominion of some strong passion." Alexander and Cæsar owed much of the force of their military talents to their ambition. Pride gave to the soul of Cato all its elevation, and vanity acted powerfully in producing the eloquence of Cicero. Avarice, when inflamed by habits of gaming, also love, anger, and all the other passions of less force, stimulate the intellects, and thereby dispose them

to evolve a greater quantity of thought. Even grief, after its first paroxysm subsides, has the same effect. The poems of Ovid and Dante, written during their banishment, the Night-Thoughts of Young, and the monodies of Lyttelton and Shaw, are inimitable proofs of the truth of this assertion. " Vexation" says Van Helmont, " brings forth understanding*." This is strictly true. Hence we seldom see young men, who begin the world without patronage or friends, rise to eminence and fame, who have not been exposed to frequent causes of irritation, from envy and malice, in early life. It would seem from this fact, that action and reaction are equal, in the strife between opposition and talents. While the former creates talents, the latter are created by opposition.

In the confessions of Rousseau there is a seeming exception to the influence of the passions in giving energy to the understanding. He says, when he was much agitated, he lost, for a while, the command of his intellectual faculties. In this case, they were stimulated beyond their power of action, by the extravagant force of his passions. The same thing happens from a great excess of stimulus upon all the moving fibres of the body.

5. The *will* should never be idle in those persons, who wish to possess great vigour and activity of mind. Slaves are stupid, because they have no wills of their own. Business, which gives the will

* Vol i. p. 470. On the power of medicine.

constant employment, should always be blended with study. It is because the pursuits of business act so powerfully in invigorating the understanding, that professional men are generally preferred for great civil appointments, to men who pass their lives among books, in a state, in which the active powers of the mind have no objects to stimulate them. It is remarkable, the faculties, after having been engaged in busy scenes, languish in retirement, and that men, who follow business of some kind, whether public or private, seldom outlive, in extreme old age, the vigour of their minds.

6. *Conversation* strengthens the intellectual faculties. Dr. Franklin acknowledged, that some of his most original ideas were suggested to him by conversing with persons, who were ignorant of the subjects upon which they instructed him. I once knew a gentleman, who wrote occasionally for the press, who made it a practice to draw his friends into a conversation with him upon the subjects on which he had been writing, before he committed his essays to the public eye; by which means, he corrected mistakes, and often added to the merit of his publications.

7. The exercise of the intellectual faculties upon *certain* specific subjects, imparts strength and activity to them. These subjects are *Politics* and *Religion*. I have elsewhere taken notice of the effects of liberty in producing the greatest quantity of animal life. It promotes the same increase of the quantity of mind. The pre-eminence of the

Greeks and Romans in intellect, over all the ancient nations in the world, was derived chiefly from the popular form of their governments. In monarchies, the birth or death of a prince, the sickness of a king, and the events of a war, are the principal objects, that, by awakening the attention of a whole nation, infuse vigour into the public mind. But in republics, the same vigour is produced every two or three years by general elections. These important seasons, in which heaven renews one of the dividing lines between man, and the brute creation, interests every feeling of the heart. They stimulate the passions, which afterwards act upon the understanding, and impart to it a force, which prevents its relapsing into the repose of public apathy, during the intervals of a general suffrage. From a strict attention to the state of mind in this country, before the year 1774, and at the present time, I am satisfied, the ratio of intellect is as twenty are to one, and of knowledge, as an hundred are to one, in these states, compared with what they were before the American revolution.

The sublime and various objects of religion are calculated to expand the human intellects to their utmost limits, and to impart to them a facility of action. We read, that the face of Moses shone, when he descended from conversing with his Maker upon mount Sinai. The contemplation of the divine character and perfections never fails to produce a similar splendour in the human mind. But

But further. It is a fact worthy of notice, that the most enlightened parts of the world, in general and useful science, are those, in which the doctrines of the Christian religion are taught and believed. Its effect, in preparing the mind for the attainment of human knowledge is happily described by Mosheim, in his Ecclesiastical History, in the following words. " The reception of Christianity," says our author, " polished and civilized in an extraordinary manner, the rugged minds of the valiant Normans; for those fierce warriors, who, under the darkness of paganism, had manifested the utmost aversion to all branches of knowledge, and every kind of instruction, distinguished themselves *after* their conversion, by their ardent application to religion and the pursuit of learning*."

8. ASSOCIATION acts powerfully upon the intellects through the medium of the memory; hence we find professional men often contract a predilection to particular situations, and objects in the prosecution of their studies. These situations from being at first imposed by accident or necessity, are sometimes in the neighbourhood of a noisy street, or in the corner of a fire-place, surrounded by a family of talking or playful children, but they are more frequently in sequestered places, remote from noise. It is from the influence of association upon the activity of the mind, that brilliant men sometimes become dull from acci-

* Vol. ii. American edition, p. 446.

dentally losing their customary chair at a club. It is from the same principle, that a boy can say his lesson best out of his own book. Even the dirt, and dogs ears (as they are called) with which it is defaced, serve to awaken the recollection of words or ideas which have been associated with them in his mind.

It might add to our knowledge of the subject before us, to mention the circumstances which diminish the force and activity of the human intellects. But these will be taken notice of when we come to treat of the remote causes of the diseases of the mind. I shall only deliver a few remarks in this place, which appear to be intimately connected with our present subject.

1st. The first is taken from Dr. Hartley. It is, that wit of all kinds, and more especially that species of it which is called punning, has a tendency to weaken the understanding by unduly exercising the imagination. Whether it was upon this account, or because persons who possessed this talent, seldom displayed it without giving offence, I know not, but I well recollect the late Dr. Wetherspoon used often to say, " that he would correct a child almost as soon for being witty, as for telling a lye." An opinion equally degrading of this talent was held by the Areopagus of Athens, and hence we read of a member of that council who resented in an open court, a detail of his public conduct in which he was said to have played upon a word.

2d. As a means of retaining the strength and activity of the intellectual faculties, no portion of them should be wasted upon unprofitable studies. We hear much of œconomy in the expenditure of money and time, but few people think of the precious nature of this excellent virtue as applied to the expenditure of intellect. The attention which is employed in reading novels, plays, and in idle conversation, carries away with it a portion of the excitability of the intellectual faculties, which can never be recovered; and thus deducts from that vigour which might have been profitably employed upon useful subjects.

3d. Several of the sources of physical influence which have been mentioned, shew us the impropriety of immuring ourselves in a cell in order to acquire knowledge. It is by the exercise of the body, and the collision of our intellects, by means of business, and conversation, that we impart to them, agreeable and durable vigour. Men may learn to *speculate* in a closet, but they will learn to *reason*, only by pursuing some active employment. There is the same difference between the knowledge acquired in the former, and latter way, that there is between the imaginary wealth acquired by speculation, and the solid property which is acquired by regular and honourable commerce.

4th. As the products of wealth by trade are always in proportion to the capital which is employed for that purpose, so the acquisition of knowledge is always in a ratio to the quantity of it which is already possessed. A few ideas upon three or four subjects impart vigour and activity only to a portion of the mind, while a large mass of ideas diffuses vigour and celerity of motion to every part of it, and thereby enables it to acquire knowledge with more facility and expedition. The degrees of vigour, and the number and exility of motions which the mind is capable of receiving by all the causes that have been enumerated, elude our present powers of calculation. Our inability to measure its attainments, will be felt more sensibly, when we reflect, that knowledge, and the intellectual faculties, will mutually increase each other, to the latest period of our lives. The effects of this action and reaction, in making additions to the intellects and knowledge, lead us to admit the assertion of Condorcet, that the time will come, when all the knowledge we now possess, will appear to the generations that are to succeed us, as the knowledge now possessed by children, appears to us. It has been said, "learned men know what is *past*, weak men what *is*, but wise men only know what is to *come*." It is possible the knowledge of what is past and present, may be so accumulated, and combined, as to render prescience, as far as is connected with our interest and happiness in this world, one of the attributes of the human mind. Perhaps this may be a part of the means that shall be made use of by Divine Providence, to produce the general diminution of evil, in our world, which is foretold in the prophetic writings of the old testament. This conjecture derives some strength from our possessing already the embryos of this kind of knowledge, in the certainty of the predictions of changes in the weather, and of the appearance, and issue of many diseases. But we must not drop this subject here. If such will be the attainments in knowledge, from the above causes, in this life, what incalculable additions to it, may we not expect, from the evolution of the same faculties, acted upon by many new impressions, in a future state of existence? Let us carry our imaginations forward, and take a view of the mind after it has continued in its renovated state ten thousand years. The difference at that period, from its most enlarged attainments in this world, will probably be much greater, than its present difference in knowledge and intellect is, from those of the meanest insect. But let us protract the period of its existence to a million of years. Here we behold a disproportion between its terrestrial and celestial states of knowledge and intellect probably equal to that which now exists between the dimensions of a grain of sand, and our globe. It would be criminal not to carry our thoughts one step further. How infinitely great must that BEING be, whose works, and attributes shall constantly furnish new objects for these constant, and growing exercises of the mind. Forever receding from them, in proportion as they are expanded, after millions of ages have revolved, the great

Father of the universe will be more and more incomprehensible, and thereby....But I forbear. The mind sinks beneath the weight of the infinite object of its future contemplations, and of its own sublime and happy destiny.

5th. From what has been delivered, gentlemen, it appears, that the enlargement and activity of our intellects, are as much within our power, as the health and movements of our bodies. This lesson has often been obtruded upon us by the entertaining spectacles of learned pigs, dogs, and several other animals. If this remark were not a just one, dulness and ignorance would not, by an innate law of our natures, be the objects of universal contempt. The aukwardness or affectation of the body, which are the effects of wilful negligence or art, are, by a similar law of our natures, treated in the same manner. Fatuity and bodily defects, which are derived from birth, or afterwards induced by disease, meet with a very different treatment from the world. They are, at first sight, the objects of universal sympathy.

6th. Many of the facts which have been mentioned, teach us, in a forcible manner, duly to appreciate the blessings of civilization, science, and religion. The innumerable stimuli, with which they abound, not only *create* mind, but from the variety and difference of force, in which they operate, they produce that variety in its forms, which renders the study and knowledge of it so agreeable and useful. A dull and disgusting sameness of mind characterizes all savage nations. Mr. Stewart, the pedestrian traveller, took some pains to establish the truth of this assertion. While in Canada, he was introduced by colonel Brandt to a number of Indian men. He asked each of them separately, why he painted himself? he said, " to look terrible in war." He then asked him, why his nation did not cultivate the arts of peace, which he described in as captivating a manner as he was capable. They appeared stupified with the novelty of the ideas he suggested, and each man answered, as if by previous concert, " that a warrior was a great man."

7th. The facts which have been mentioned, serve further to refute the objection which has been urged against the Mosaic account of the whole human race being descended from a single pair, from the weakness of the intellects in certain savage and barbarous nations. This weakness is as much the effect of the want of physical influence upon their minds, as a disagreeable colour and figure are of its action upon their bodies.

I shall conclude our lecture by remarking, that much remains yet to be known upon this subject. It is possible, the strength of the intellects may be improved in their original conformation, as much as the strength of the body, by certain mixtures of persons of different nations, habits, and constitutions, in marriage. The mulatto has been remarked, in all countries, to exceed in sagacity, his white and black parent. The same remark has been made of the offspring of the European and North American Indian. The physician, whose name, and long residence in the East-Indies, were mentioned in another place, informed me, that the marriages of Danish men, with the East-India women, produced children, that had the countenances and vigorous minds of Europeans, but that no such results appeared in the children of marriages of East-India women with the males of any other European nation. Similar facts may be very common, but not observed. It is probable, the qualities of body and mind in parents, which produce genius in children, may be fixed and regular, and it is possible, the time may come, when we shall be able to predict, with certainty, the intellectual character of children, by knowing the specific nature of the different intellectual faculties of their parents. As conjugal happiness, in its positive degree, is often the result of dissimilar tempers, so, strong intellects in children, may be the product of a difference in the mental faculties of the two sexes. There is one fact, which favours this opinion. A late French writer has remarked, that judgment in one parent, and a predominance of imagination in the other, produce, in their offspring, the most perfect and well-balanced minds.

8th. In the former part of this lecture, I took notice of the effects of certain liquors in invigorating the mind. May there not be some production of nature or art, yet undiscovered, that shall act in such a manner upon the brain, as to enlarge and strengthen the intellectual faculties, so as to enable them to accommodate to difficulties and emergencies, in the contemplative and active pursuits of life? Kempfer tells us, that he was treated with a liquor, in Persia, called Peganum, which produced suddenly, the most extravagant sensations of joy. They continued, he says, for three days, and then left him, with an oblivion of all he had said and done, during his paroxysm of mental delight. Perhaps there exists upon our globe, a substance, which shall produce similar transports in the excitement and exercises of the intellectual faculties. This conjecture is rendered probable, by a fact, related by Ettmuller. He tells us, that he had known three cubebs taken every day, to have a wonderful effect in invigorating the memory. Should this boon be reserved for the human race, it will be humane and pious to wish, that it may not be found out, until men shall cease to concentrate the utmost force of their faculties, in discovering new modes of private and public oppression, and new instruments for inflicting pain and death upon each other.